The Mysteries copyright © 2023 by Bill Watterson and John Kascht. All rights reserved. Printed in China. No part of this book may be used or reproduced in any manner whatsoever without written permission except in the case of reprints in the context of reviews.

Andrews McMeel Publishing
a division of Andrews McMeel Universal
1130 Walnut Street, Kansas City, Missouri 64106

www.andrewsmcmeel.com

23 24 25 26 27 TEN 10 9 8 7 6 5 4 3 2 1

ISBN: 978-1-5248-8494-9

Library of Congress Control Number: 2023931229

ATTENTION: SCHOOLS AND BUSINESSES
Andrews McMeel books are available at quantity discounts with bulk purchase for educational, business, or sales promotional use. For information, please e-mail the Andrews McMeel Publishing Special Sales Department: sales@amuniversal.com.

The Mysteries

Story by
Bill Watterson

Pictures by
John Kascht and Bill Watterson

Andrews McMeel
PUBLISHING®

www.andrewsmcmeel.com

The Mysteries

Long ago,
the forest was dark and deep.

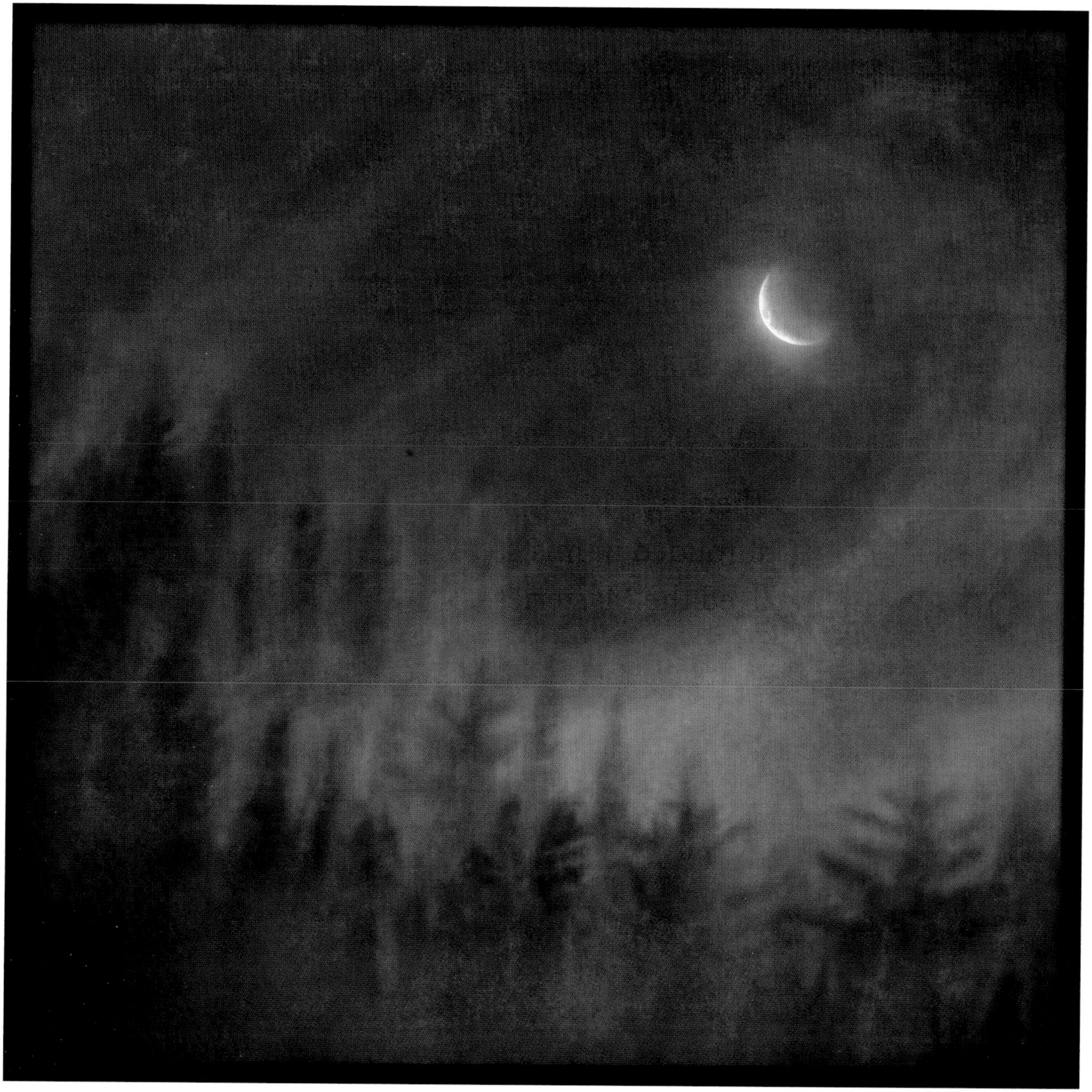

There,
shrouded in mists,
lived the Mysteries.

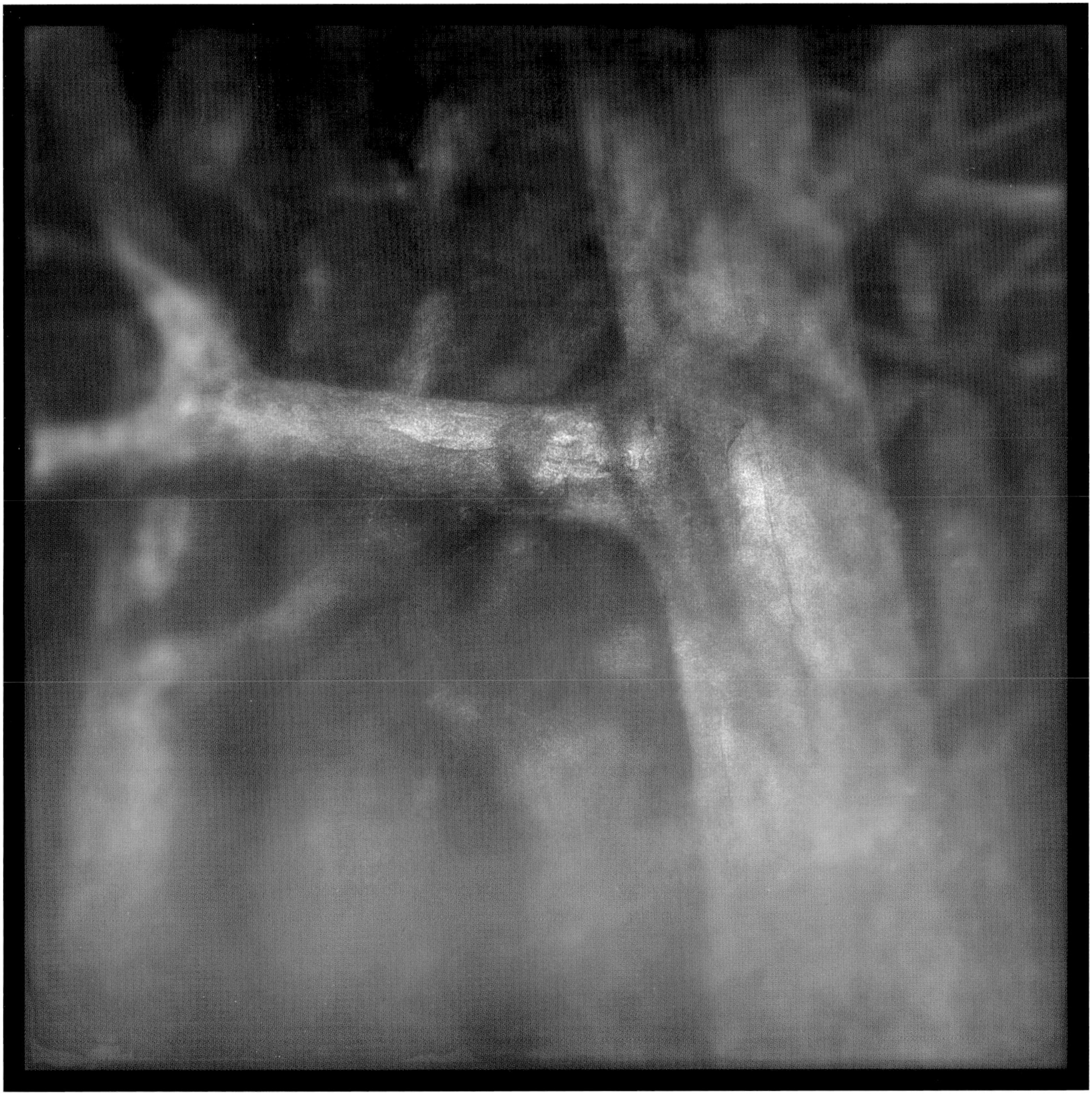

Nobody had ever seen them,
but they seemed to be everywhere.

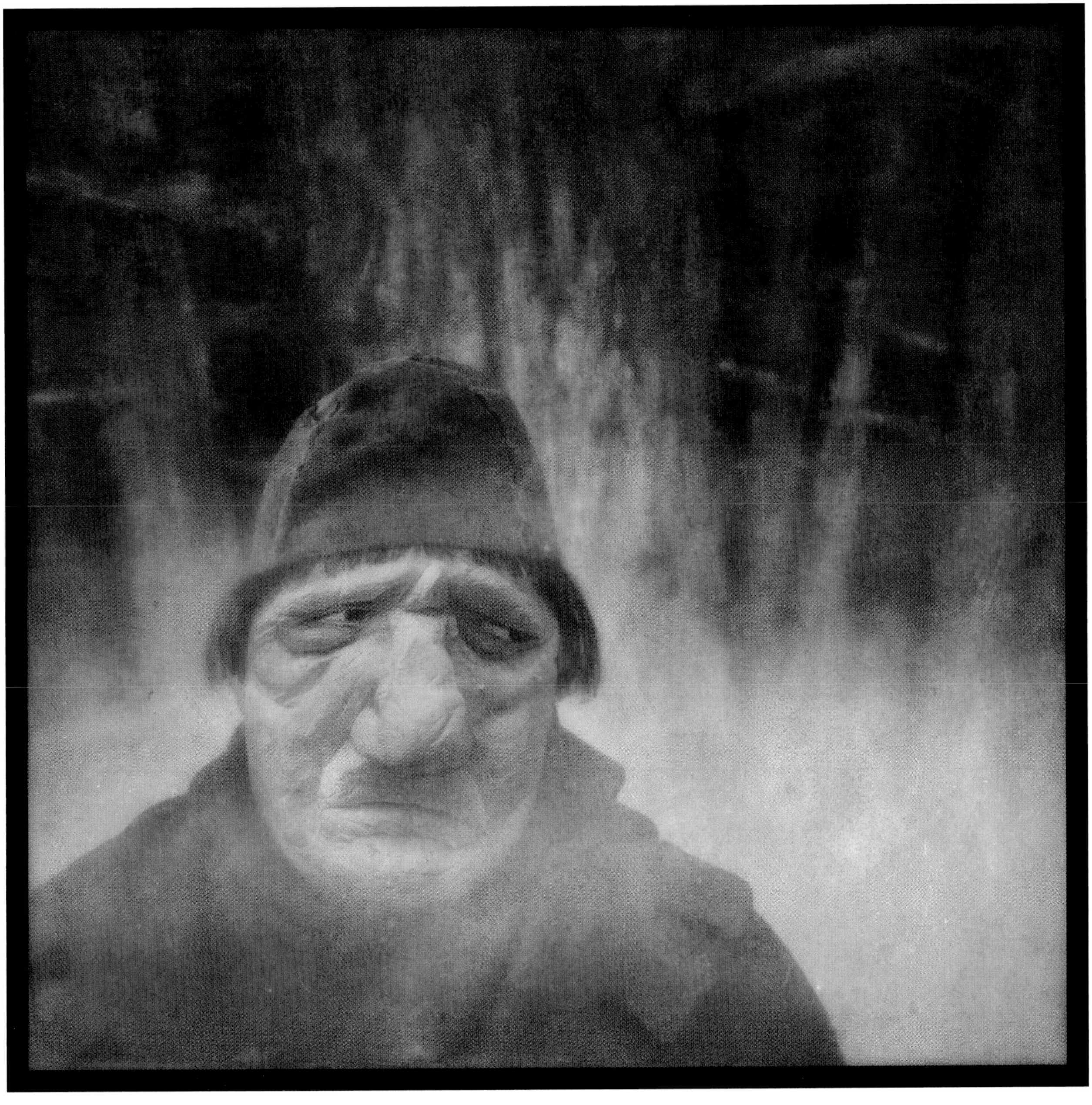

And the people
lived in suspicion and fear.

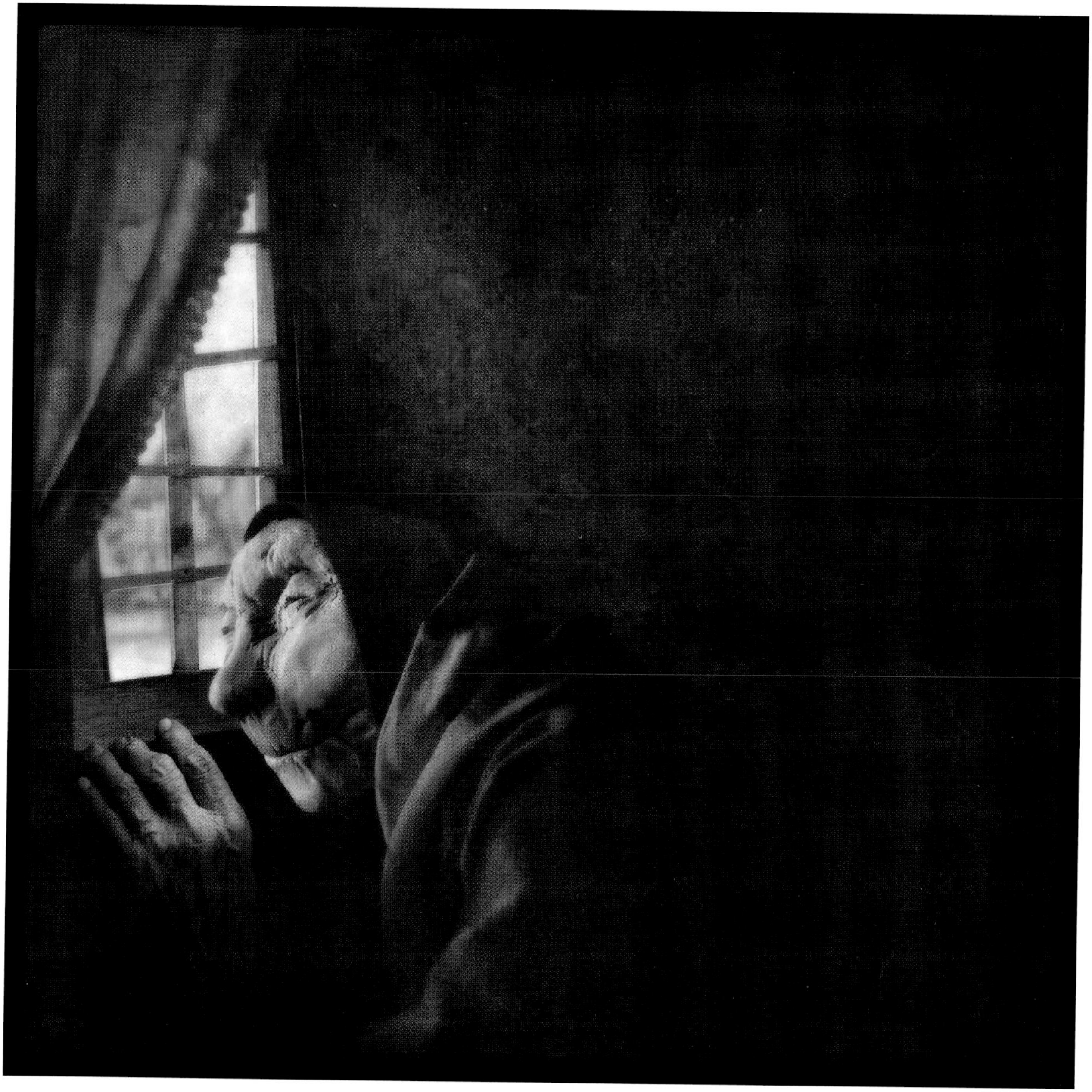

To protect themselves,
the people built enormous walls.

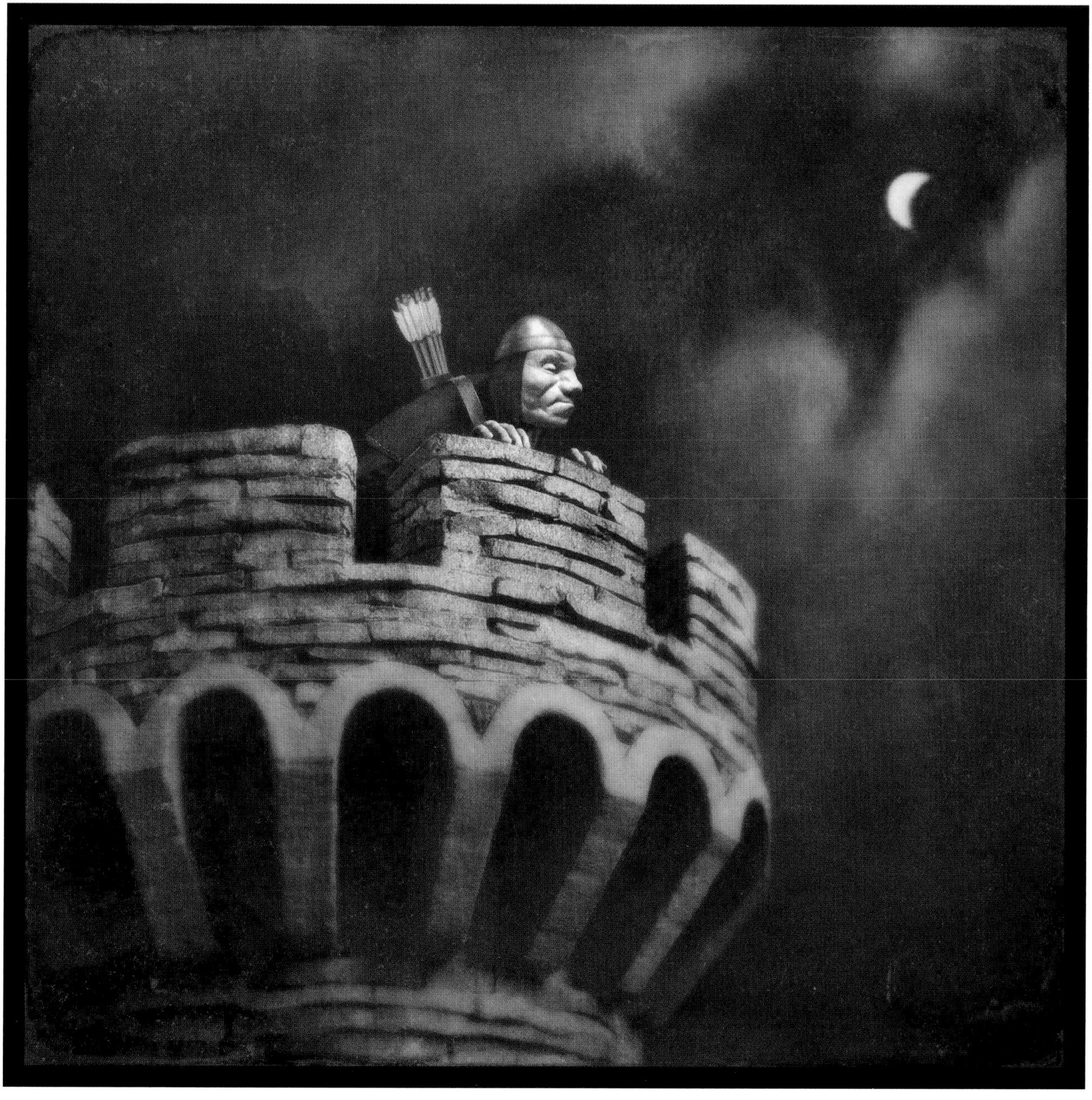

And within those walls,
storytellers told of the Mysteries'
bizarre and terrifying powers.

Artists depicted the people's
many sufferings.

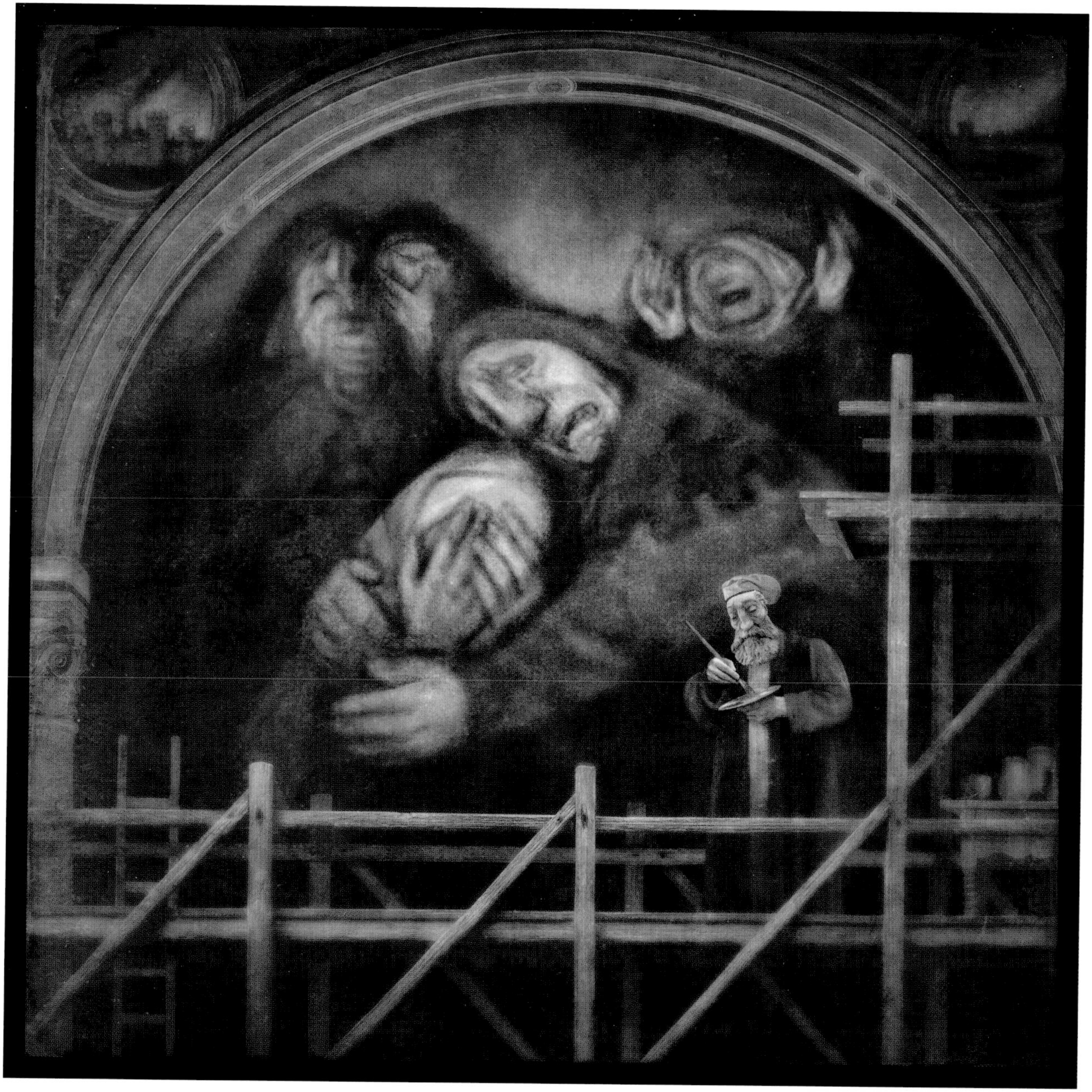

"If only we could be rid
of these horrible Mysteries,"
people whispered,
glancing over their shoulders
and hurrying on.

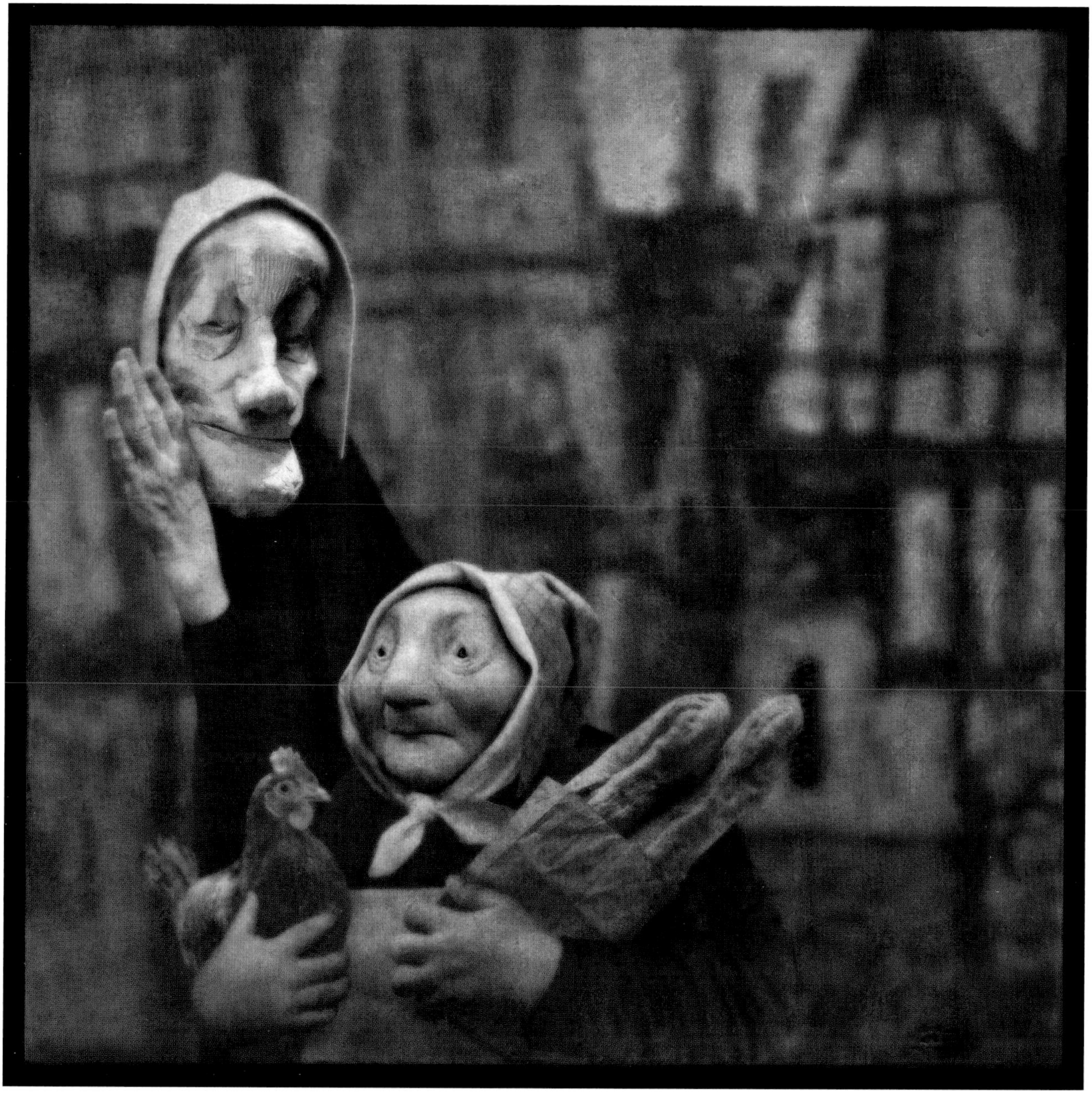

But every day,
things happened for which
there were no explanations.

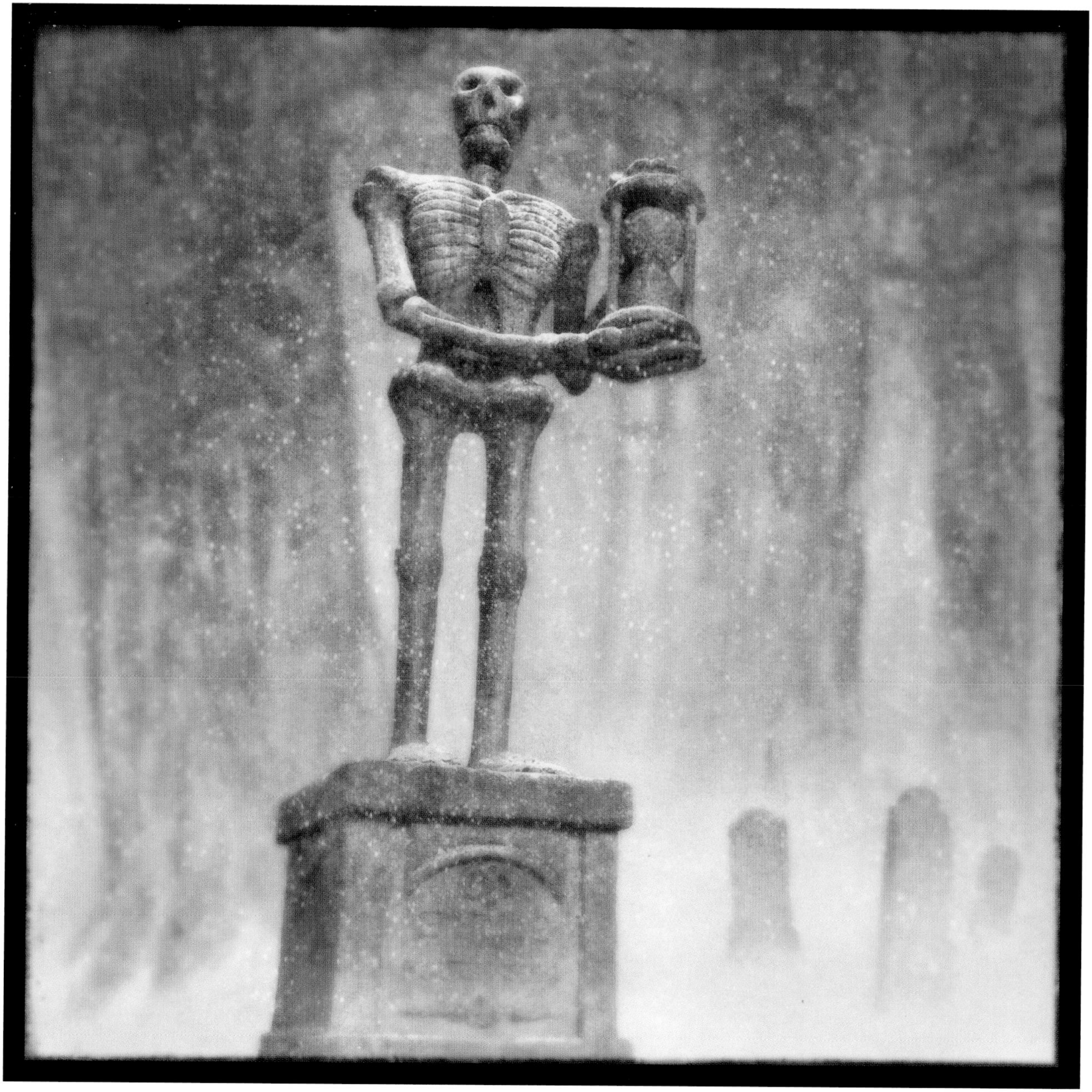

These were frightful times.

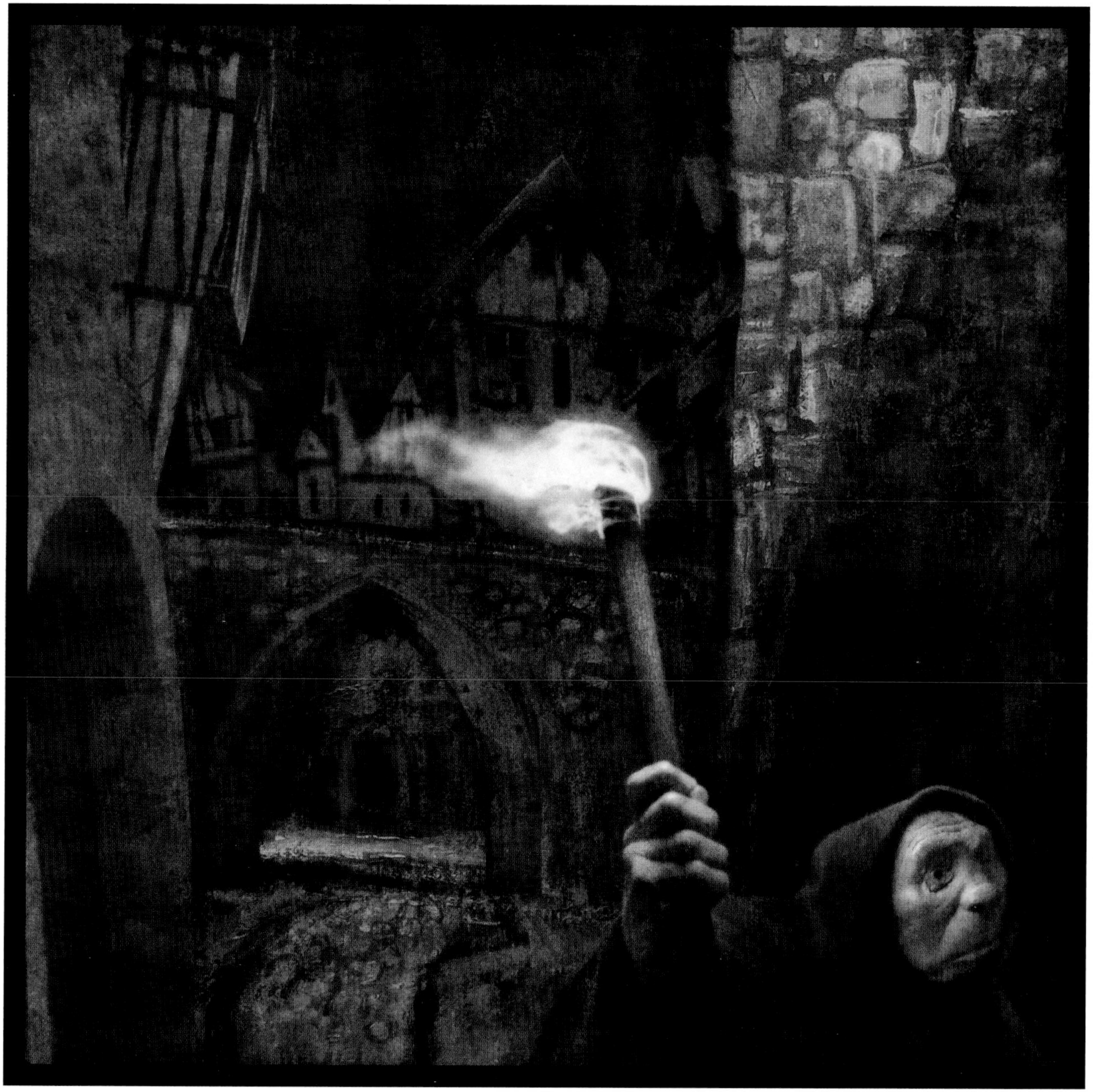

Finally, the desperate King
summoned his Knights
and ordered them
to capture a Mystery.

Perhaps the Mysteries' secrets
could be learned, and their
powers could be thwarted.

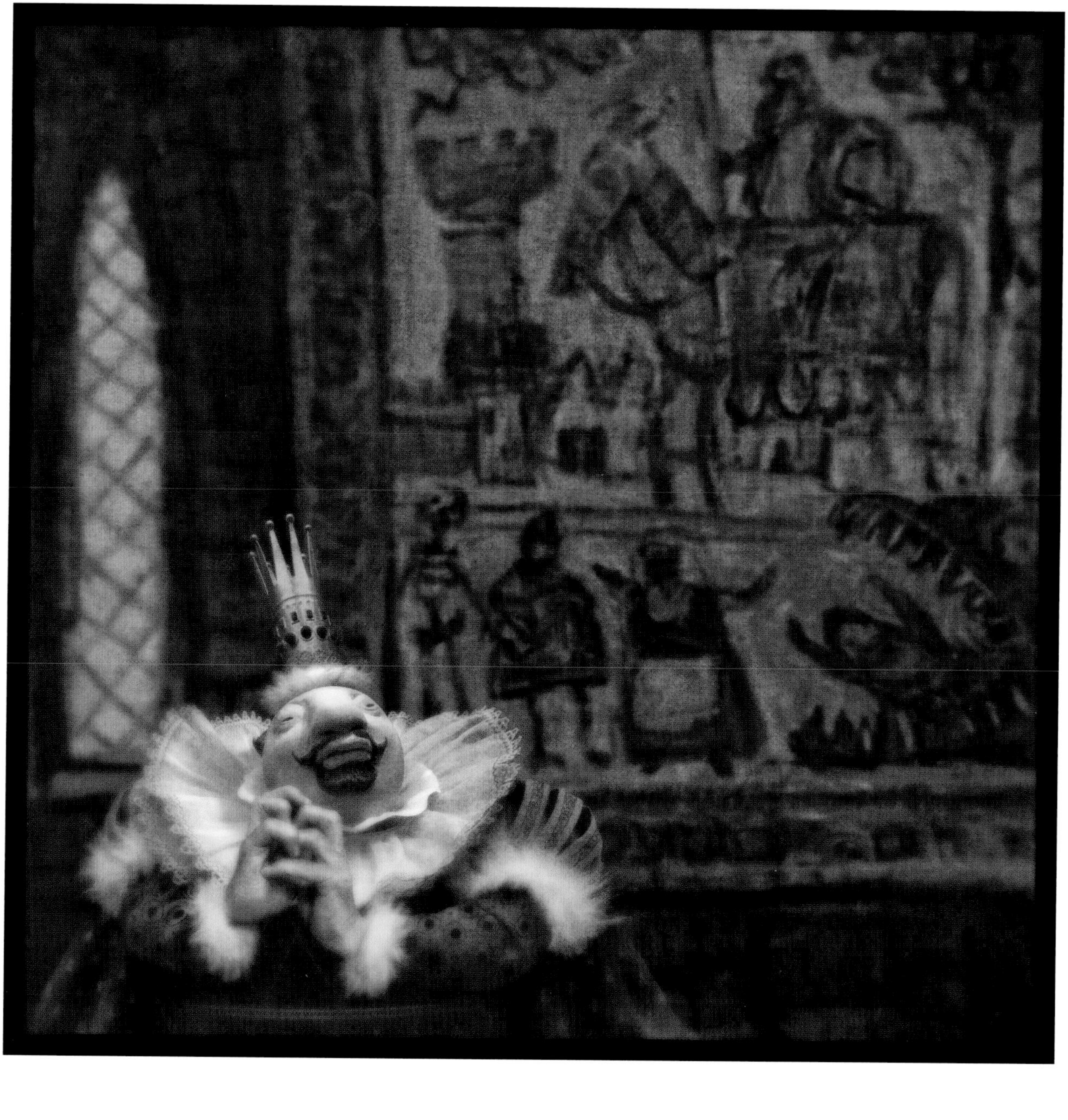

So the Knights set off
into the misty forest.

Year after year they searched.

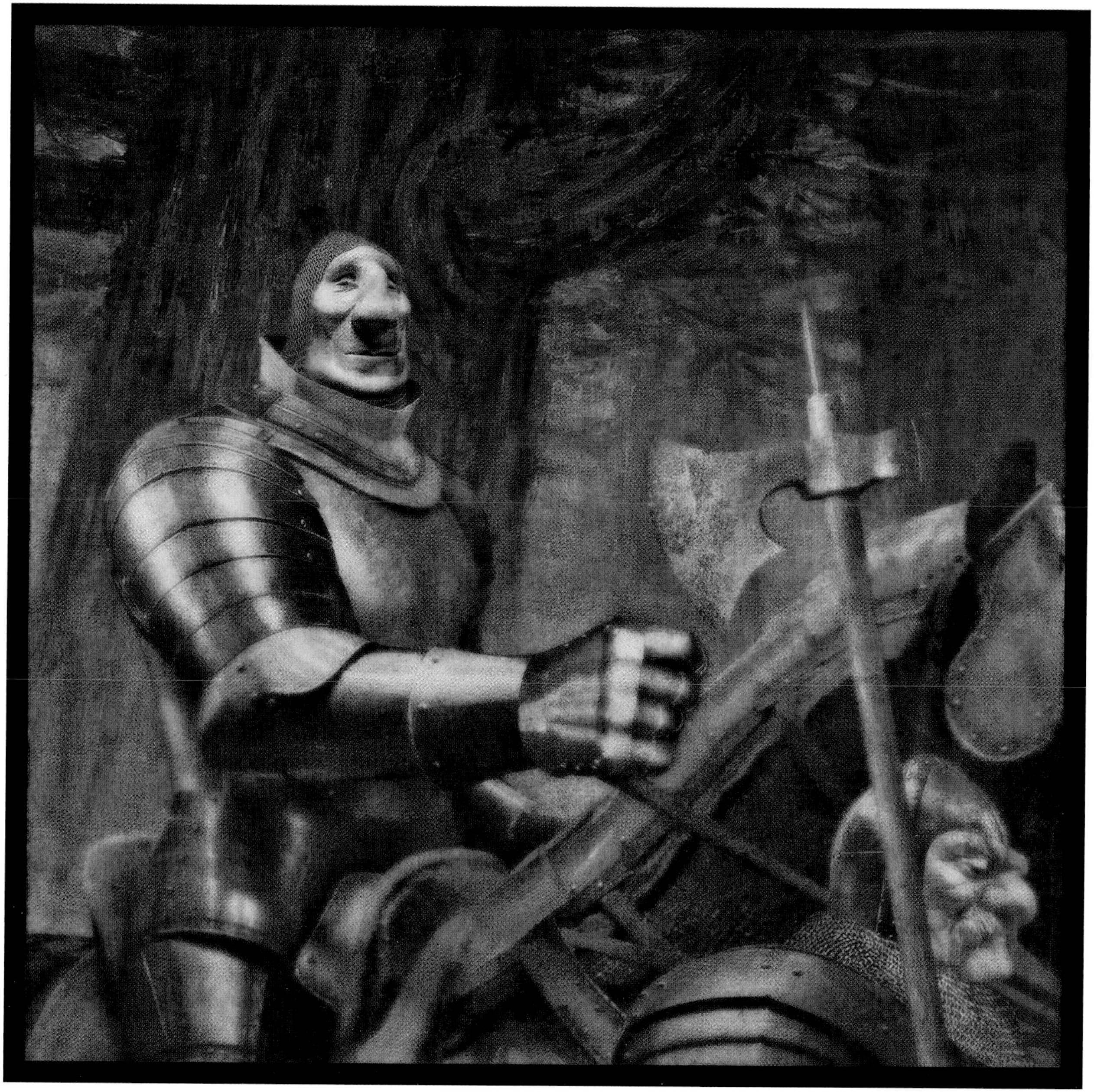

Many Knights were never seen again.

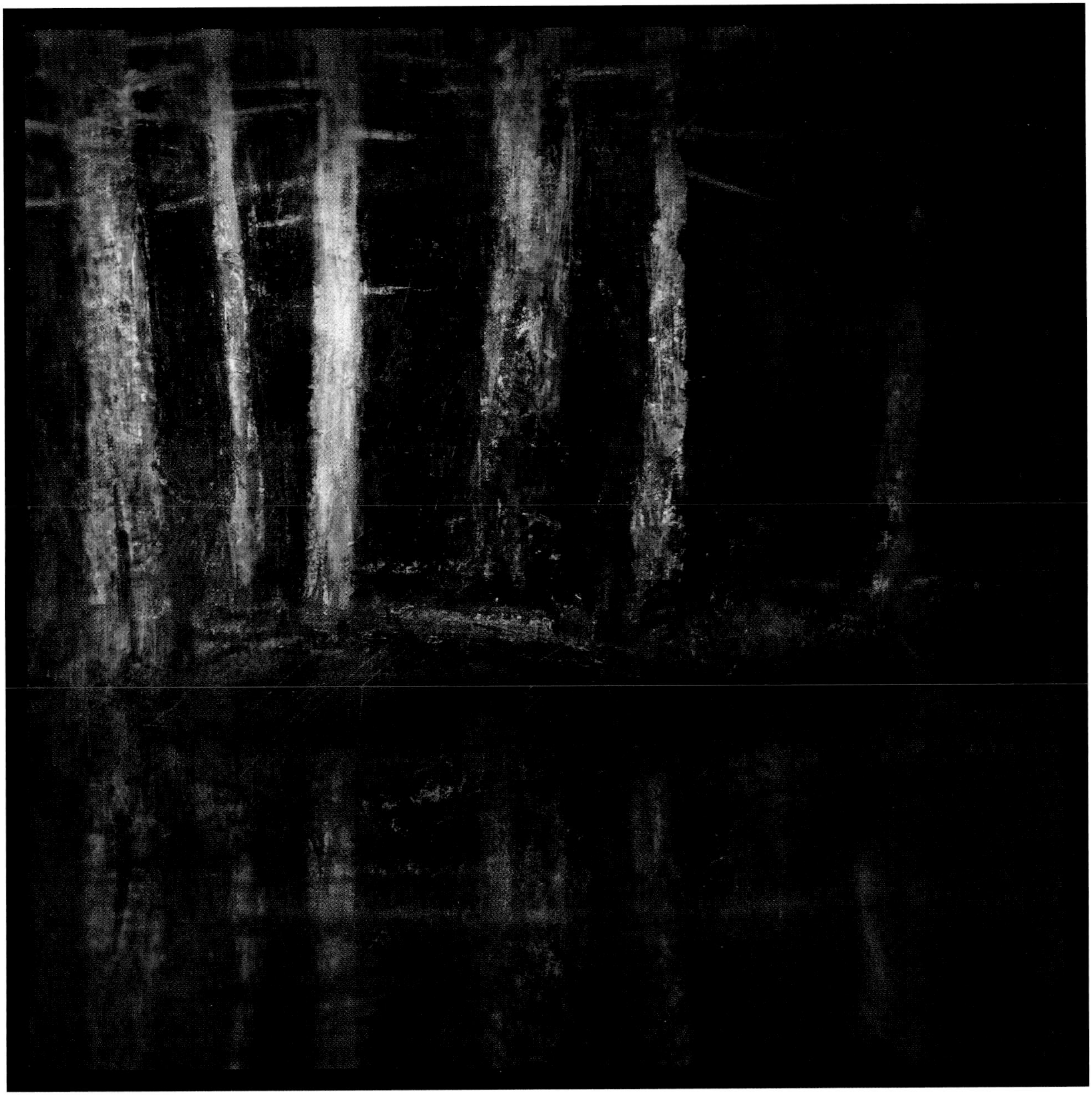

But eventually,
one dazed and exhausted Knight
staggered back to the King.

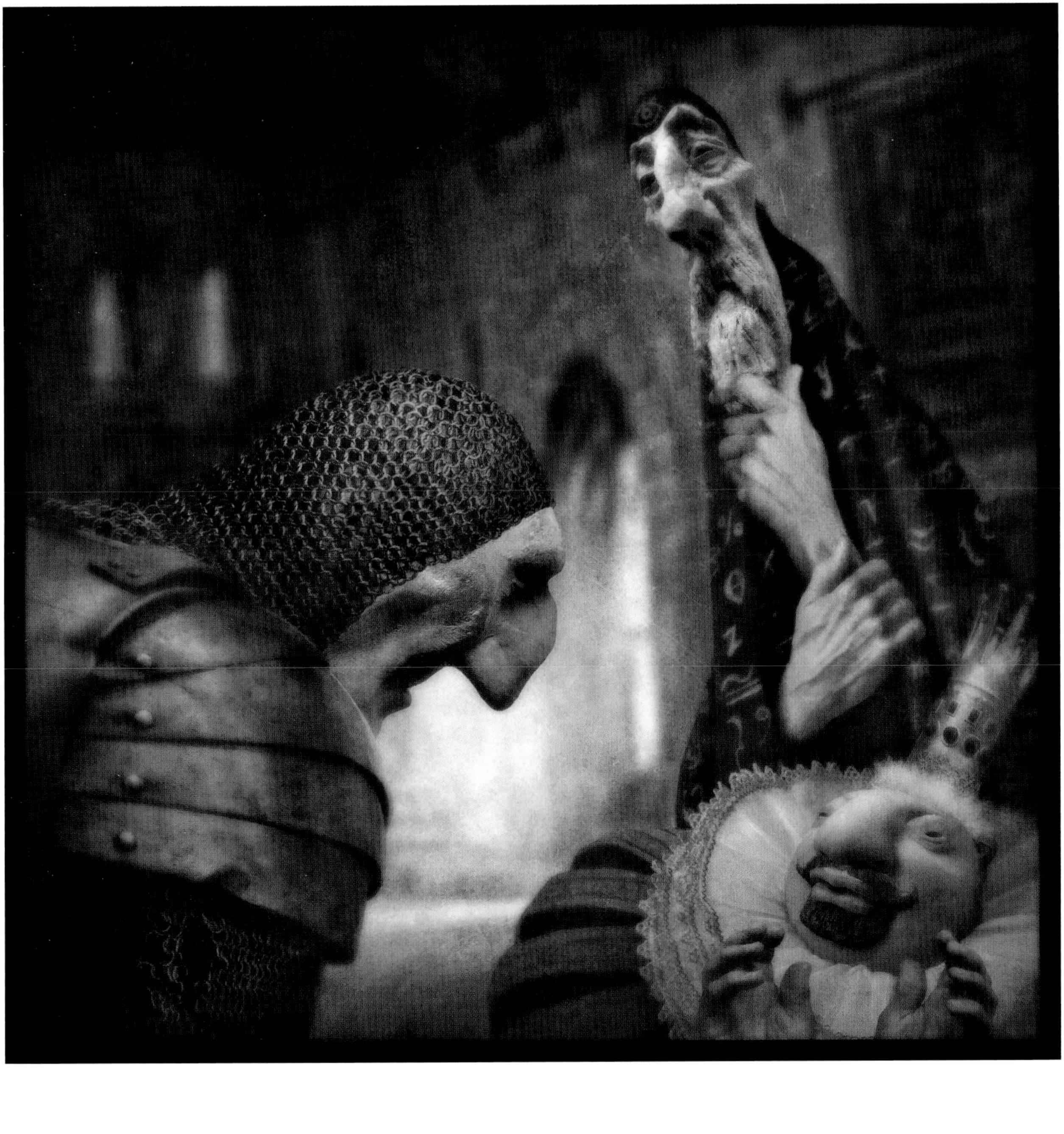

A Mystery had been captured!

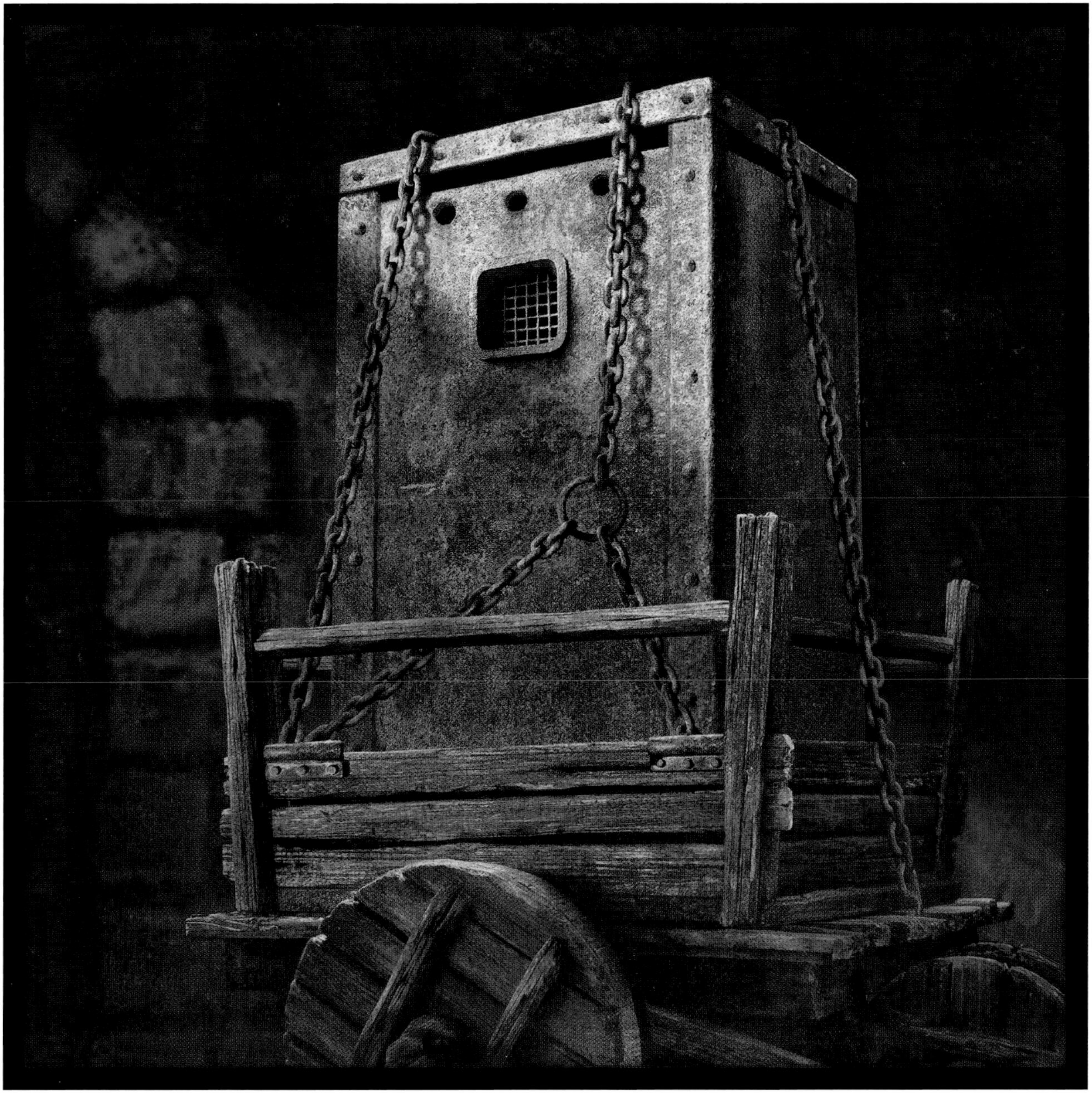

The public thronged
to the great unveiling.

But the Mystery was nothing
like what the ancient stories
had led the people to expect.

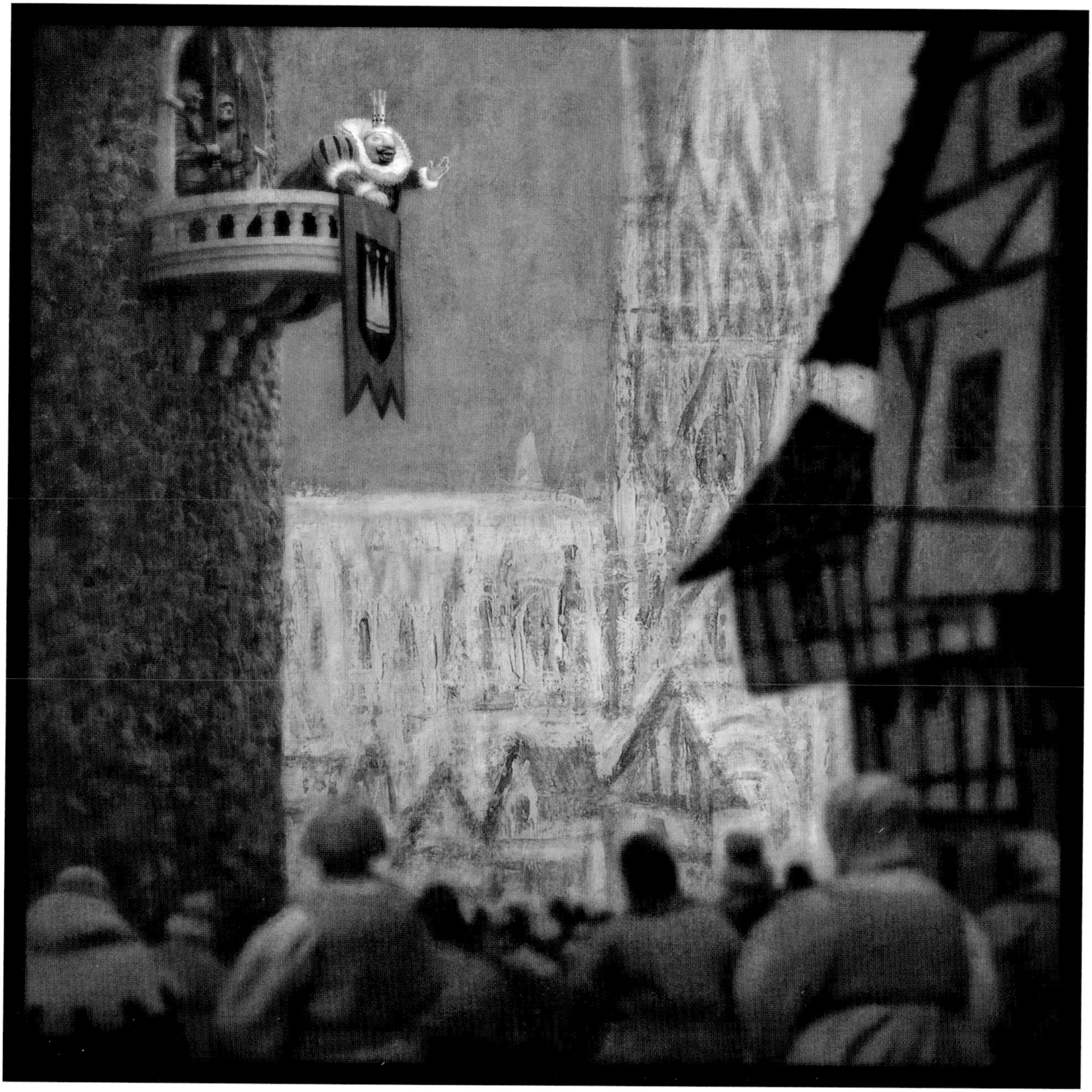

The people were stunned.

The Mystery
looked surprisingly ordinary.

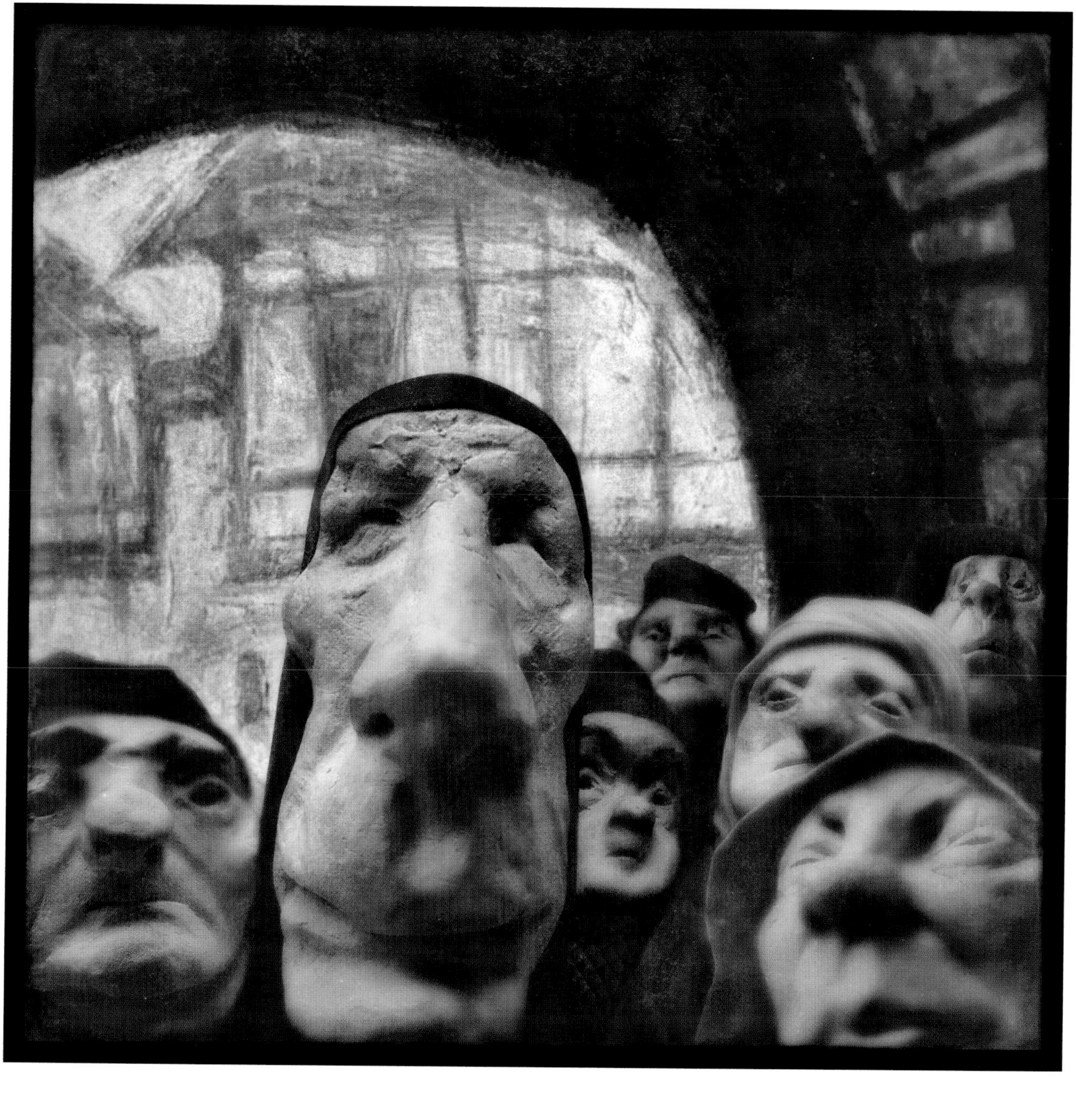

Once understood, its powers
were not all that remarkable.

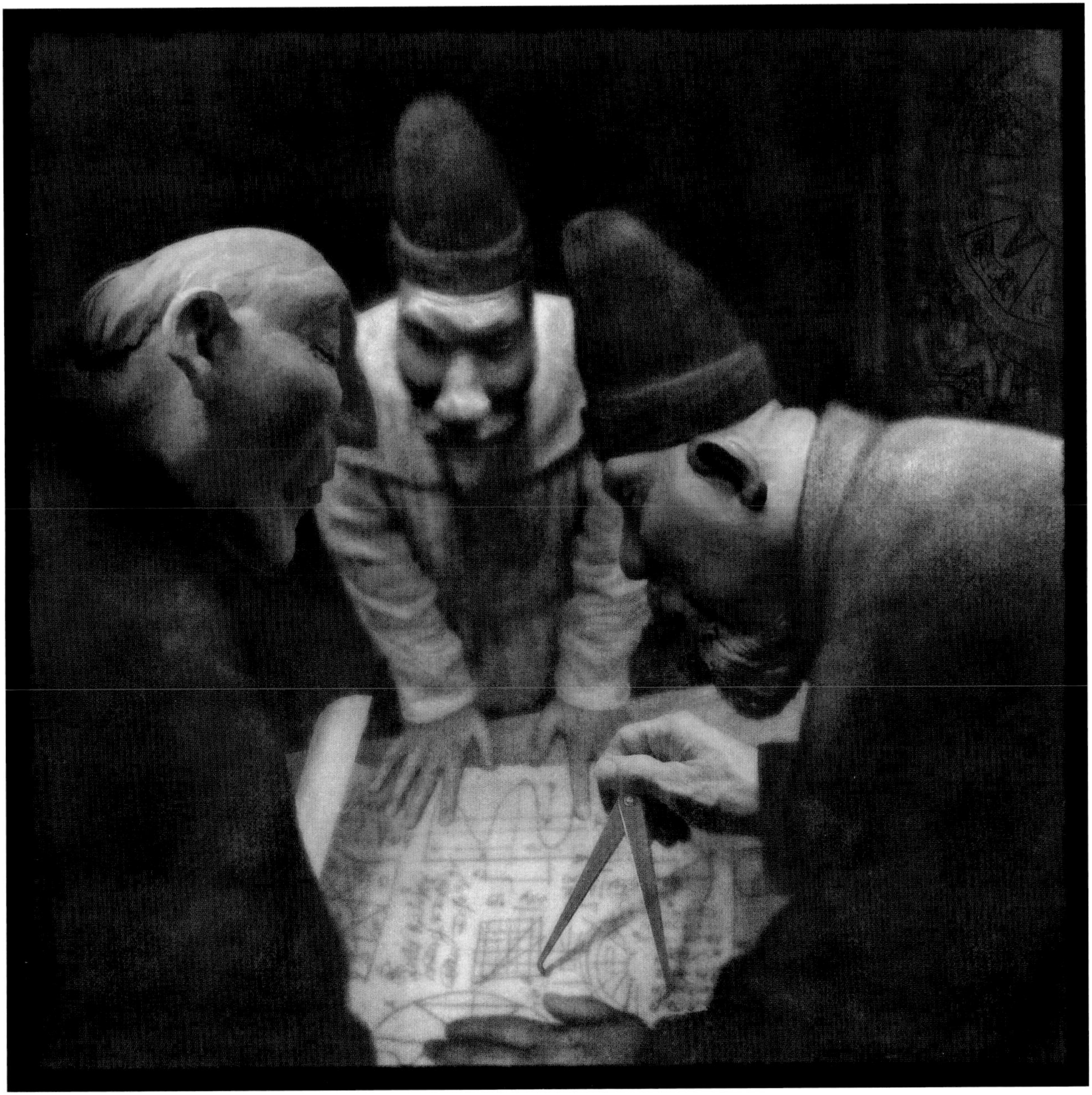

And over time,
each new Mystery they discovered
was even less impressive.

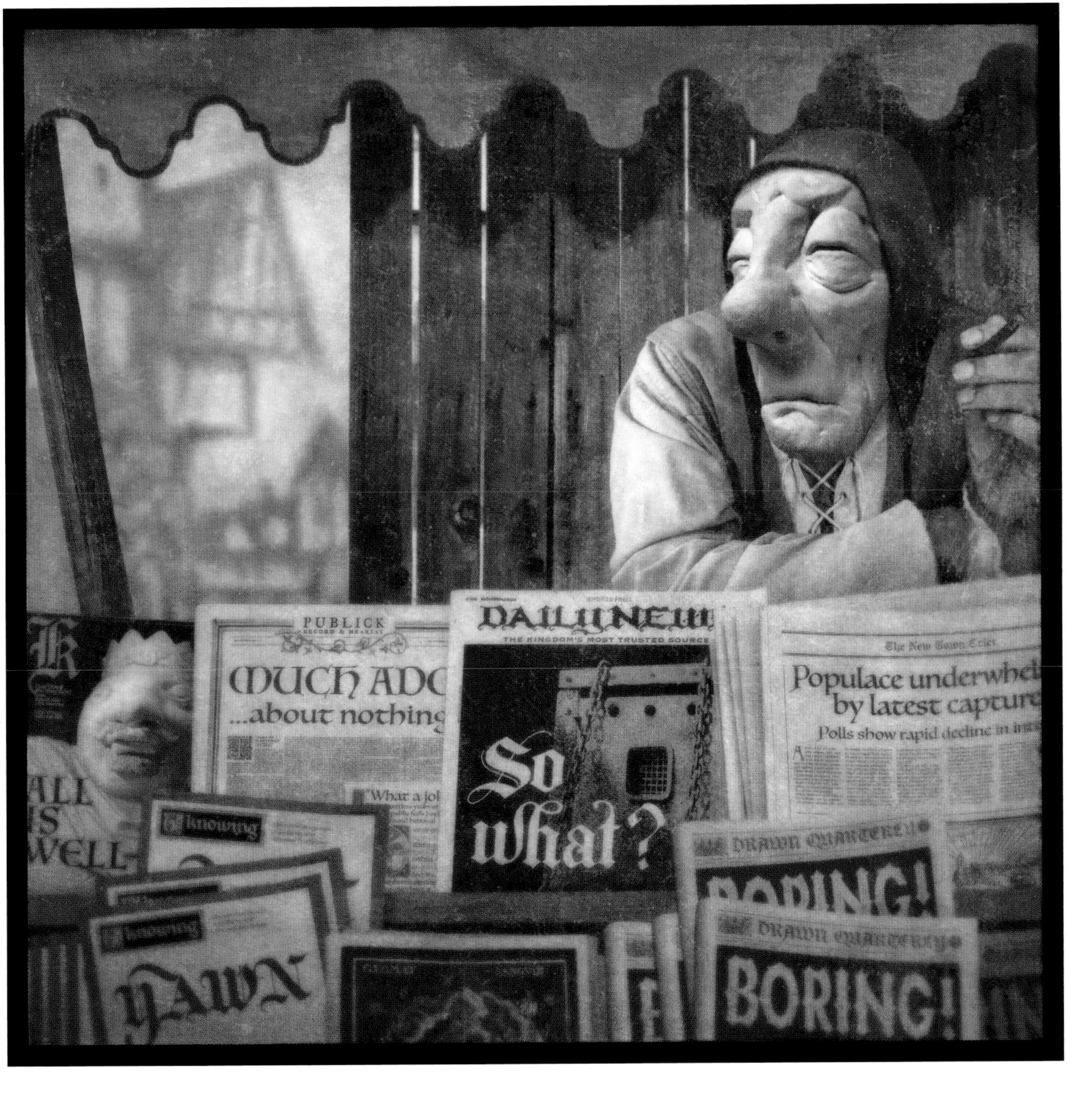
PUBLICK
THE KINGDOM'S MOST TRUSTED SOURCE
...about nothing
So what?
by latest
Polls show rapid decline in
BORING!
BORING!
YAWN

Gradually the people stopped
fearing the Mysteries.

They laughed at the old paintings.

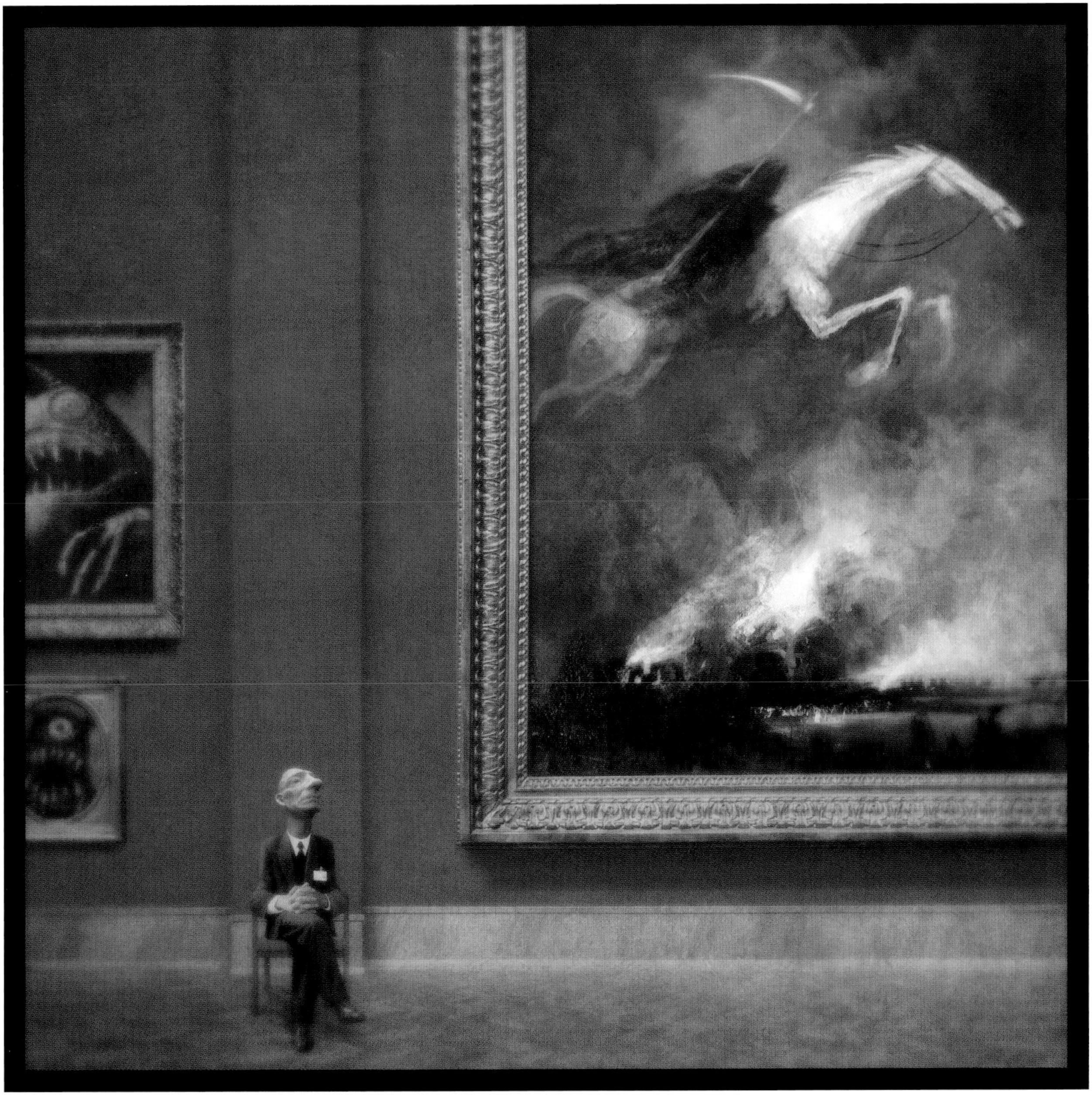

Soon, the great walls were dismantled
and the forest was cut down.

The people spread across
the once-fearsome land.

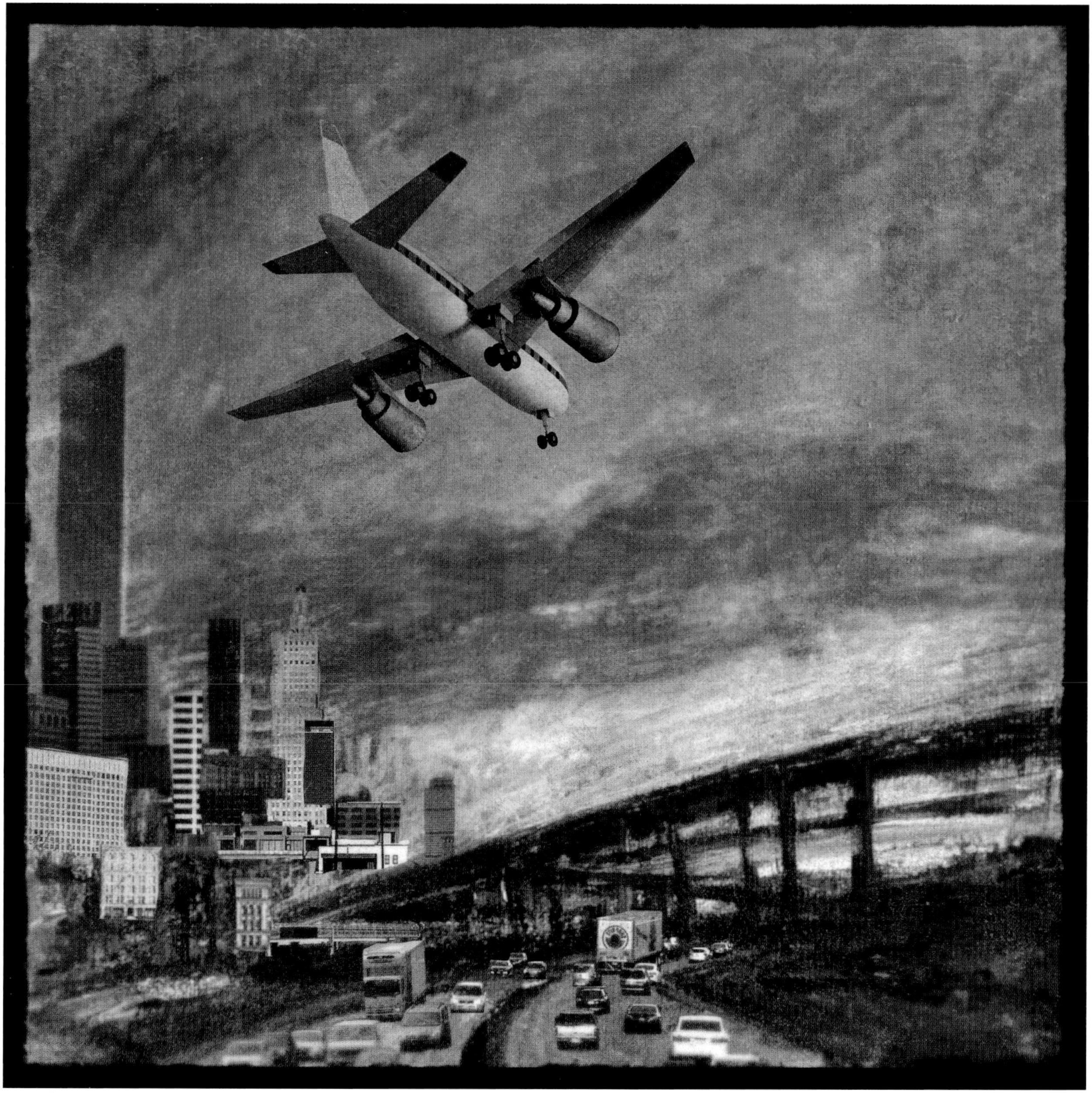

The Mysteries vanished,
and the people lived luxuriously.

They were finally
in control of everything.

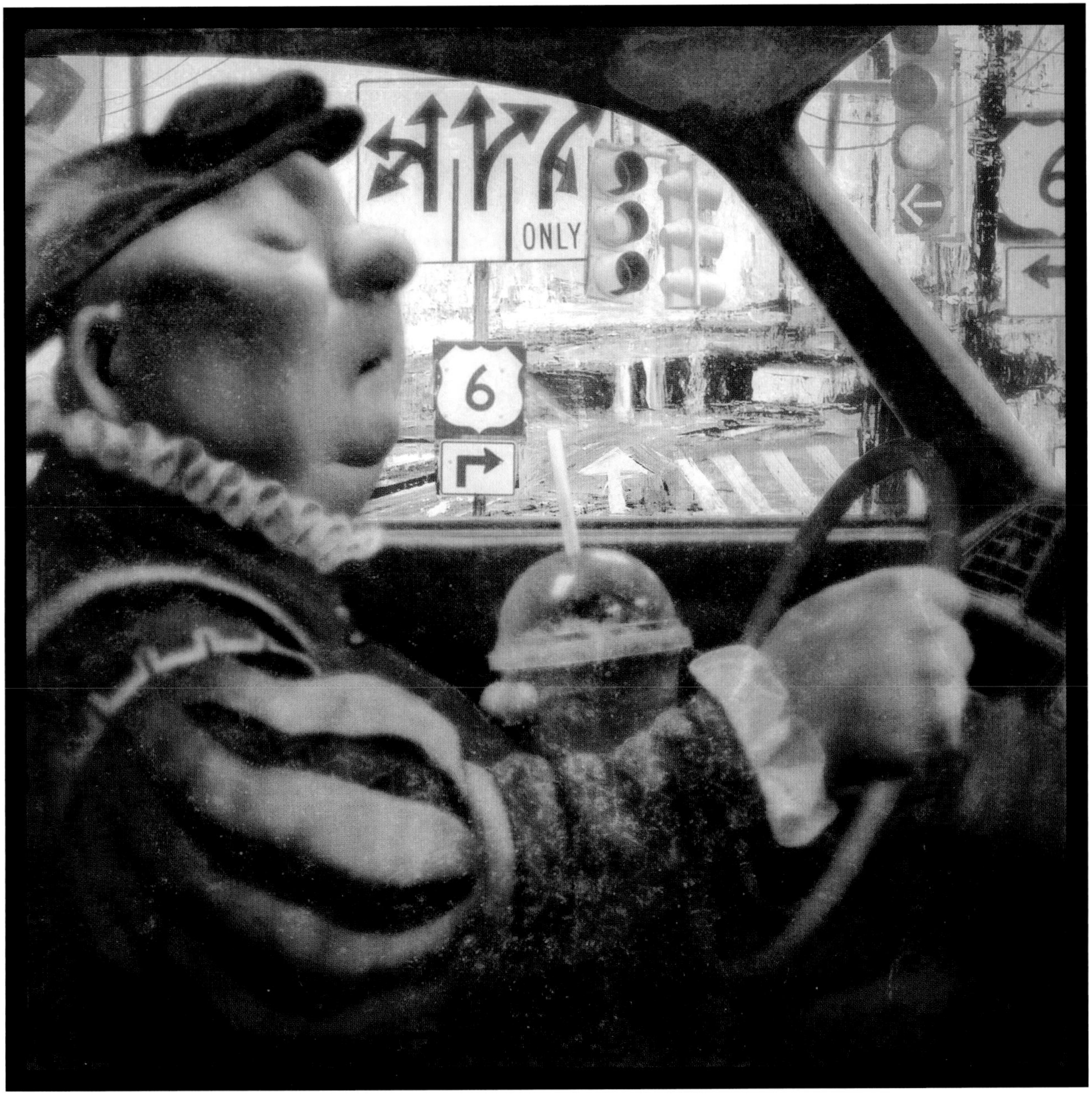
ONLY
6

By and by however,
the sky turned a slightly weird color.

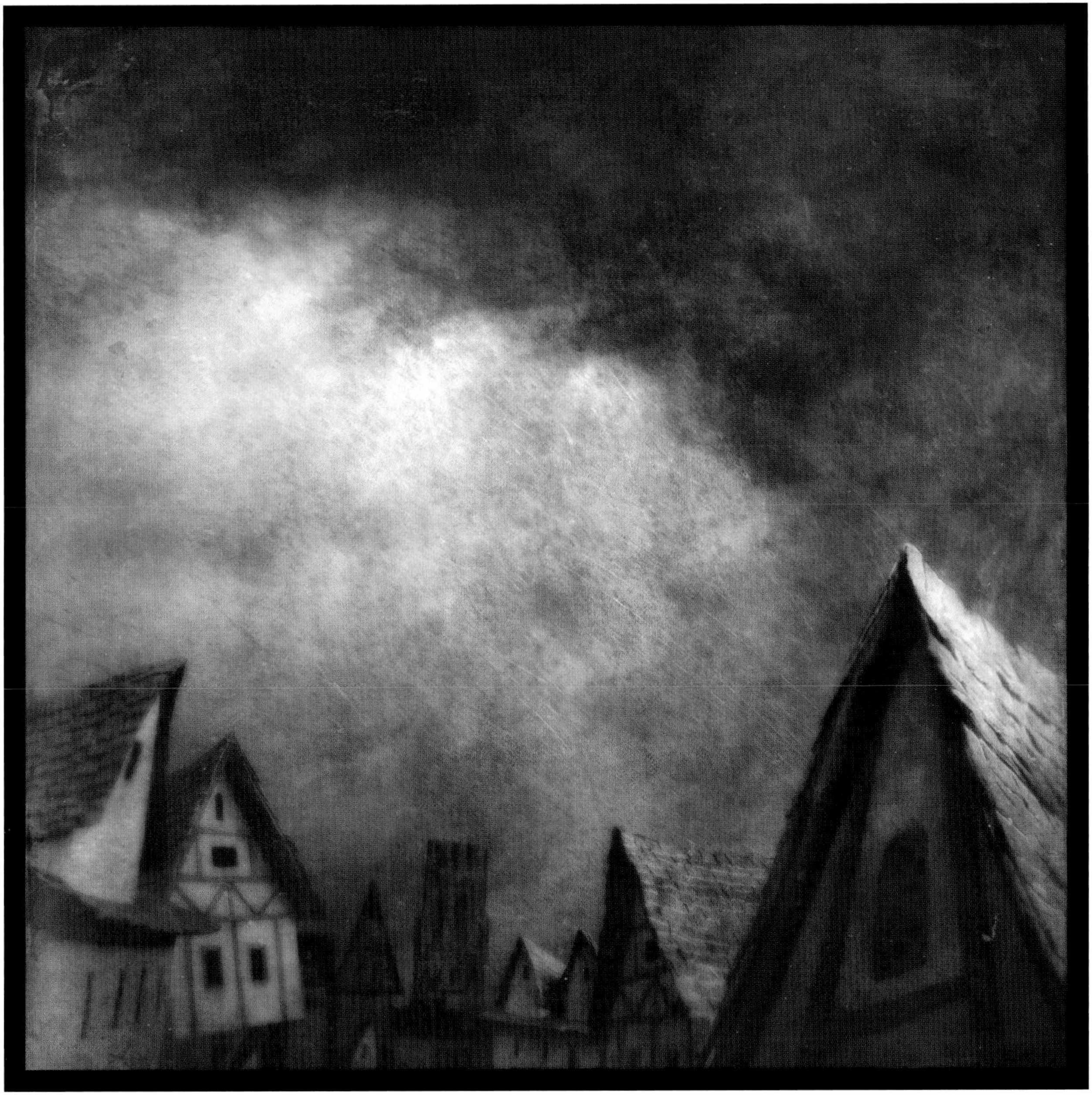

People wondered about it,
but the King assured everyone
that this was a perfectly
normal variation.

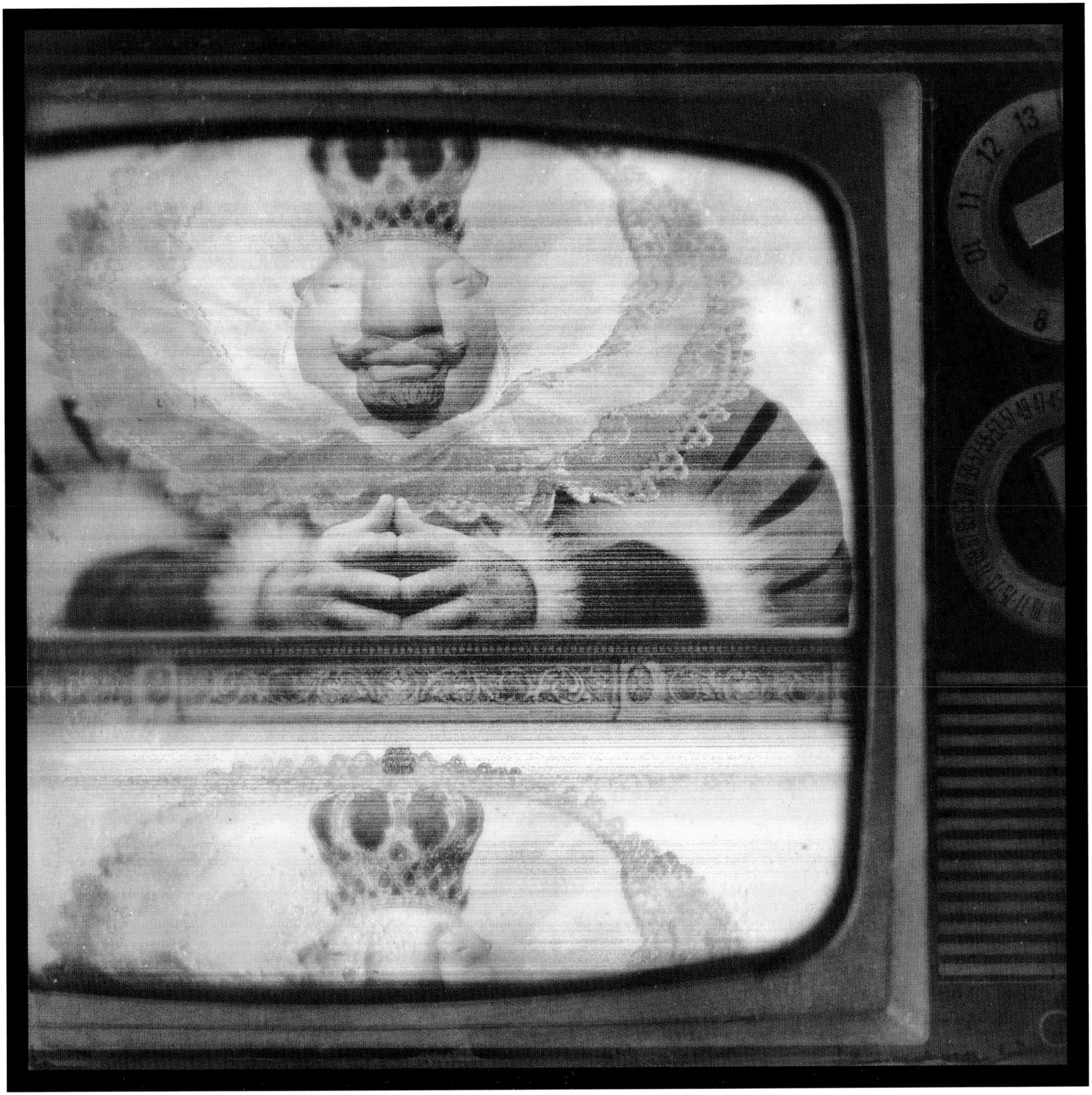

Nevertheless, the Wizards
watched the horizon uneasily
and made note of the
strange creaks and shudders
occurring far below in the ground.

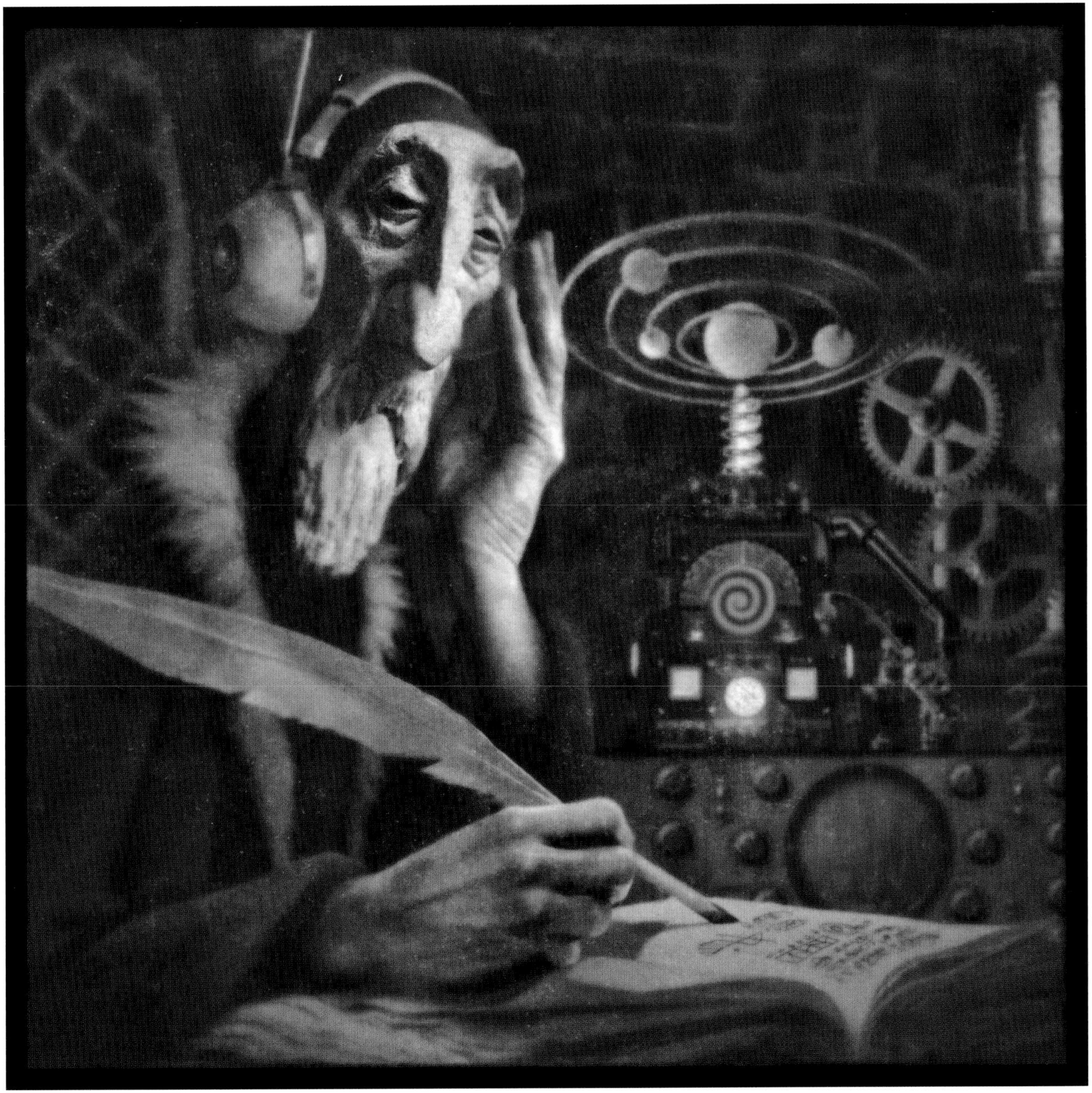

Acrid smells drifted in
from across the seas.

Sometimes flaming objects
fell from the sky.

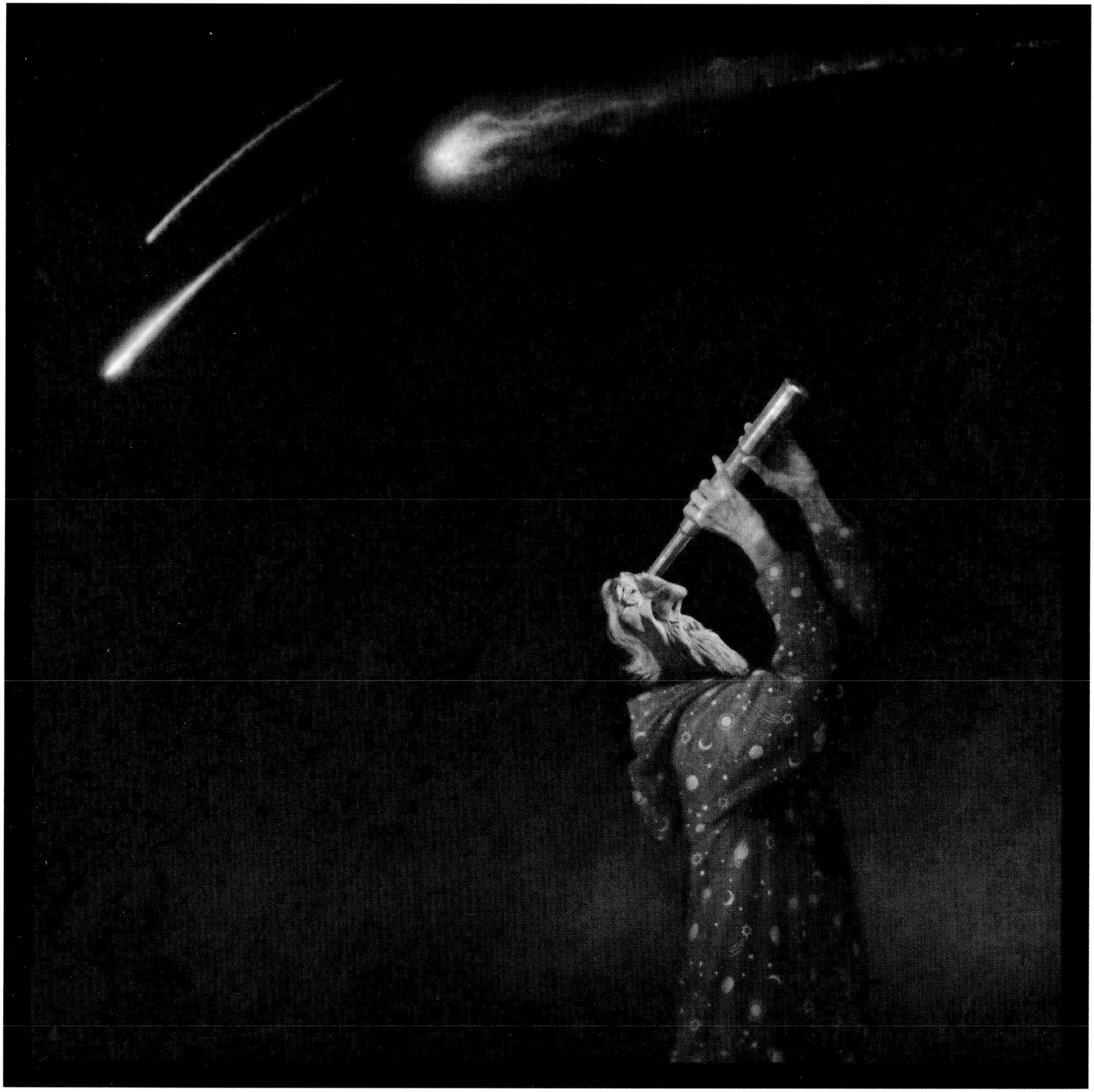

Animals started migrating
to remote corners of the earth.

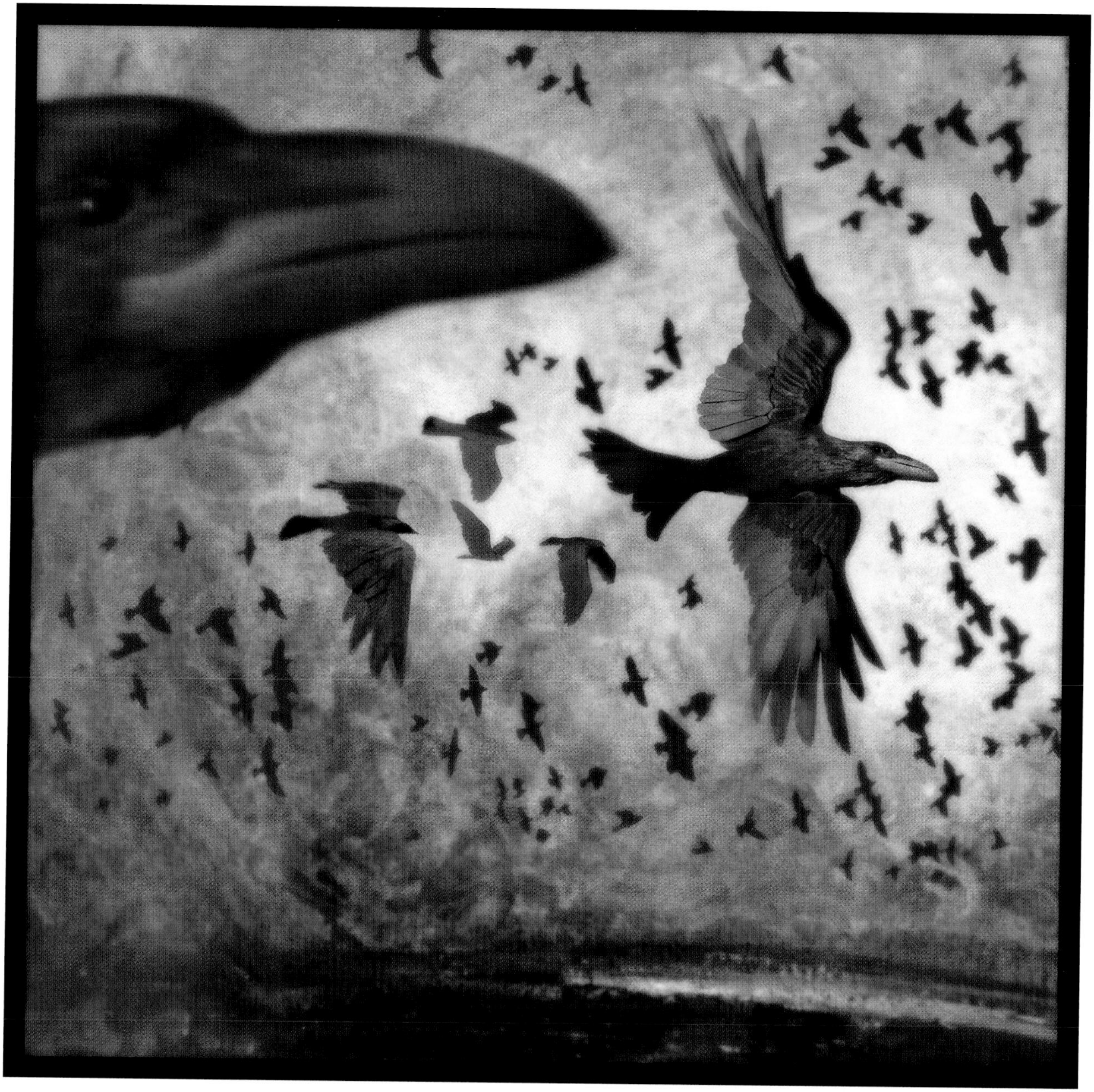

The scouring winds
became more persistent.

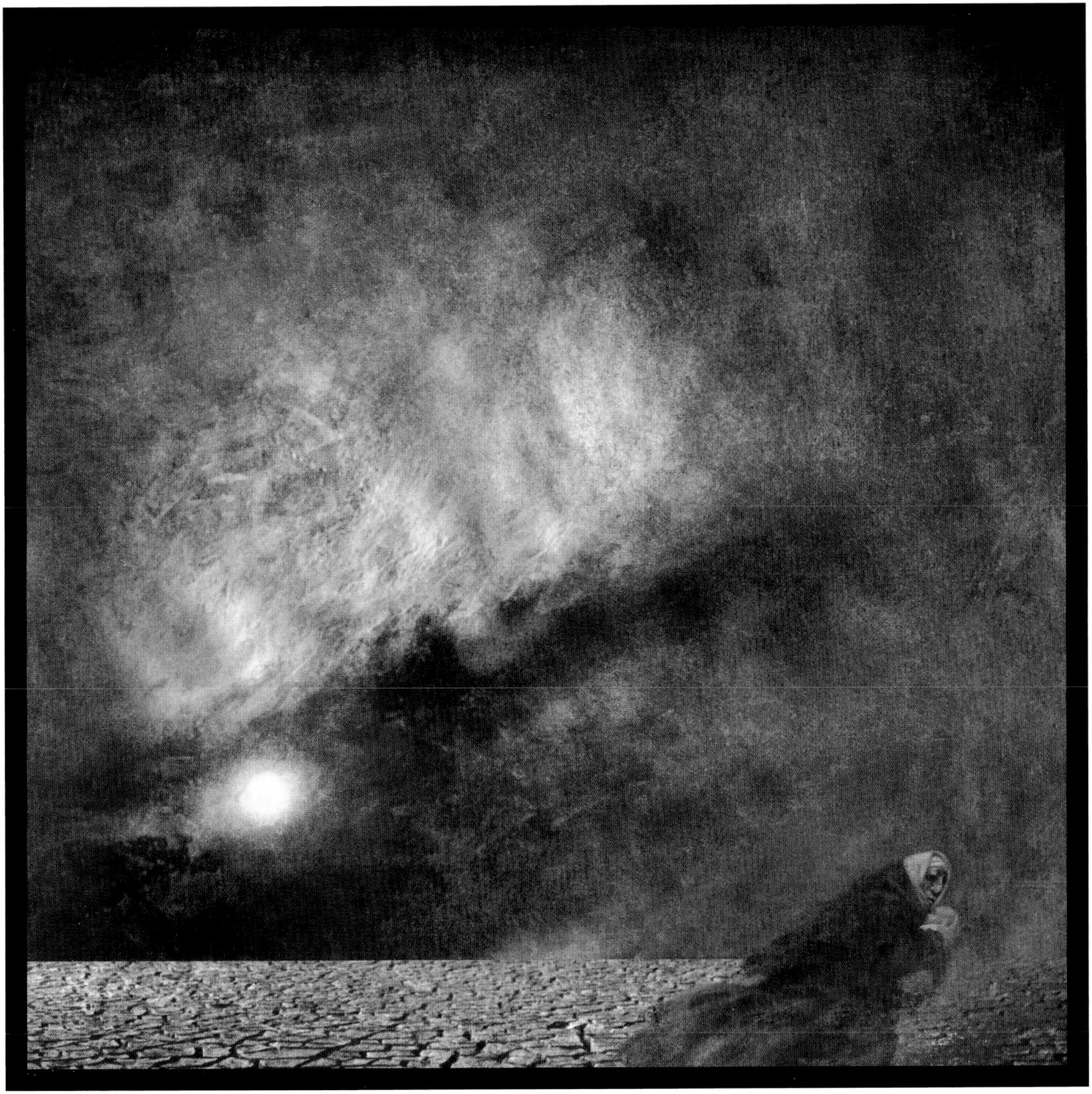

And more and more often,
things disappeared.

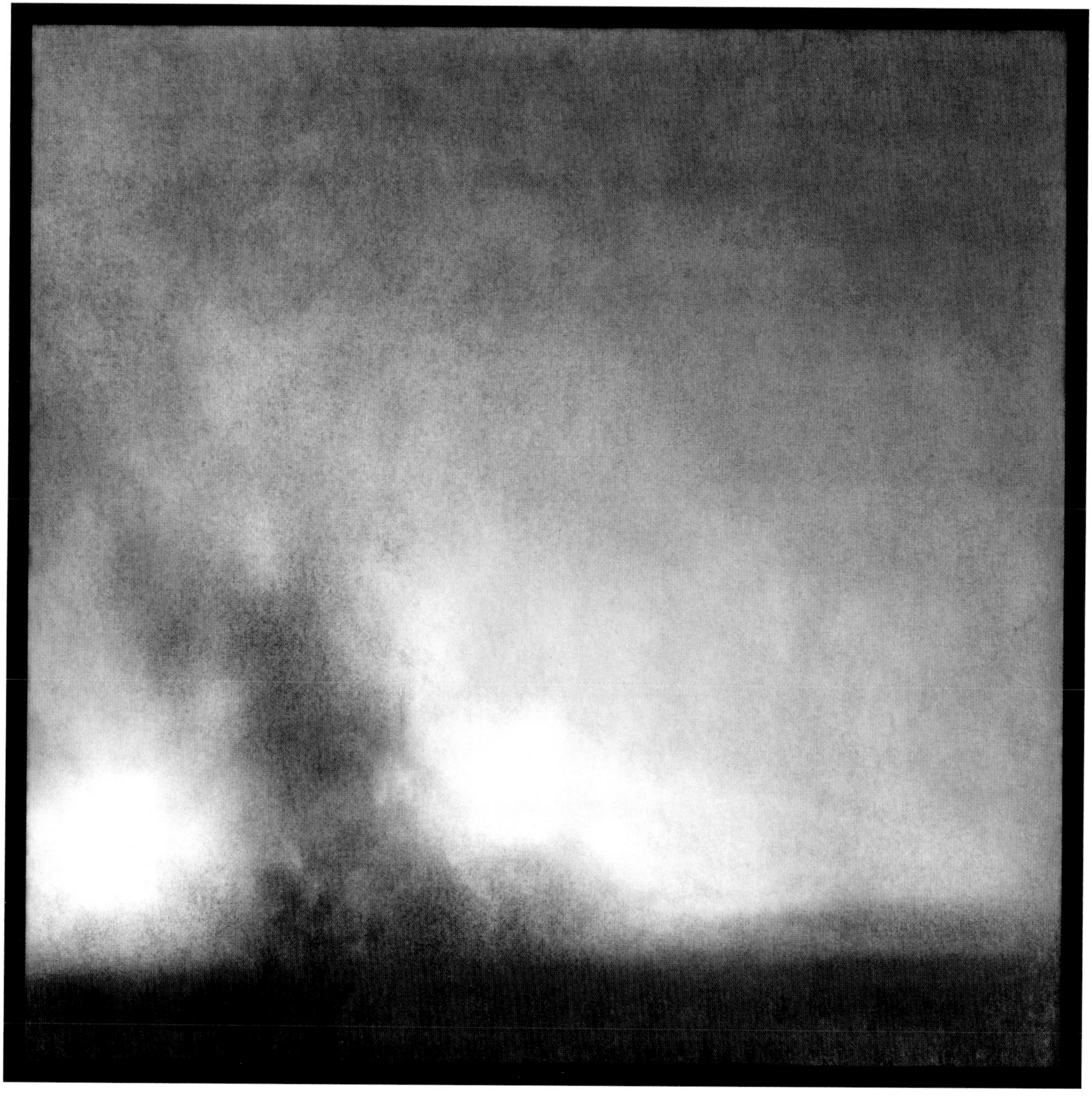

Rather late,
the people grew alarmed.

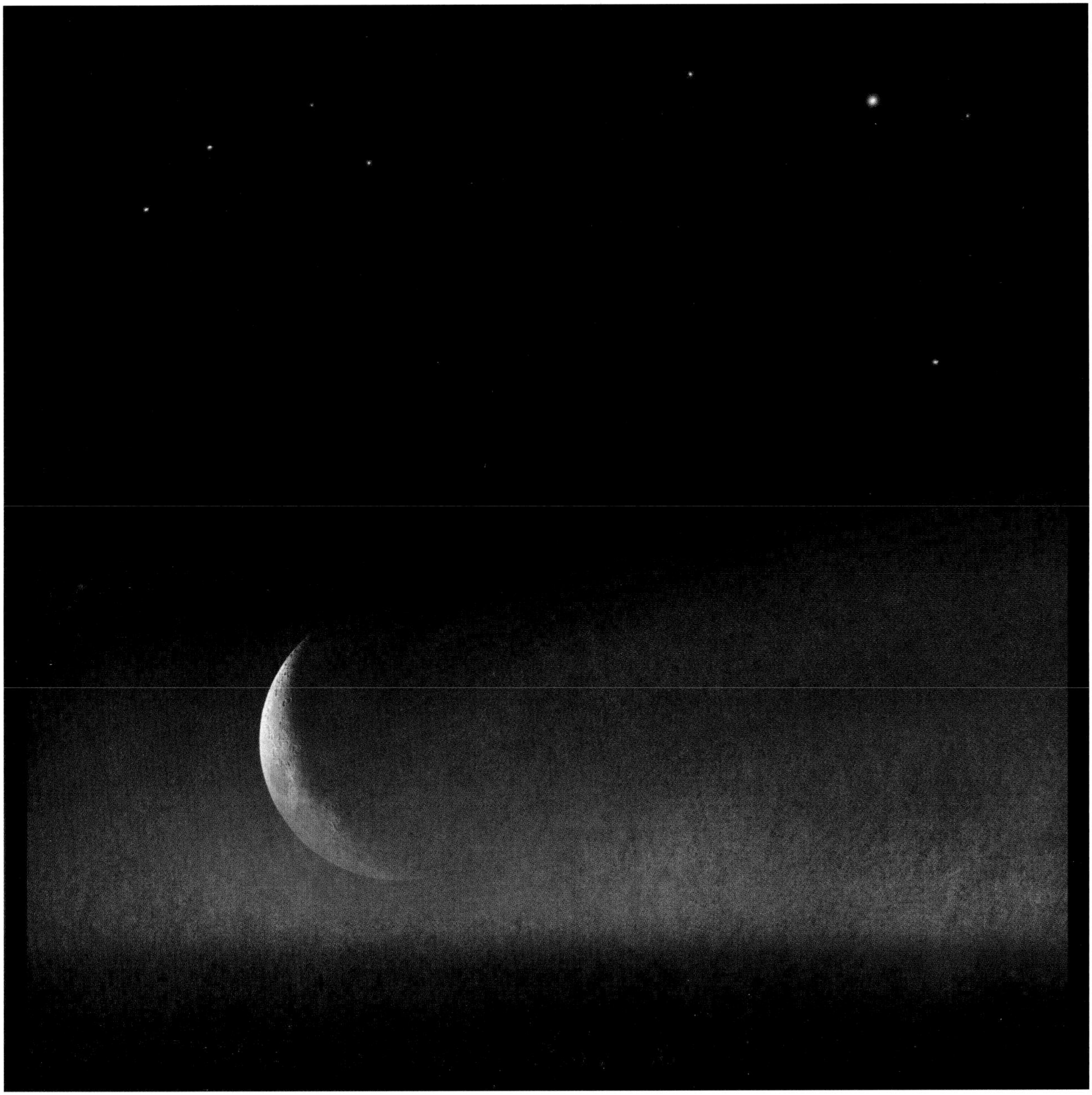

Time moved on.

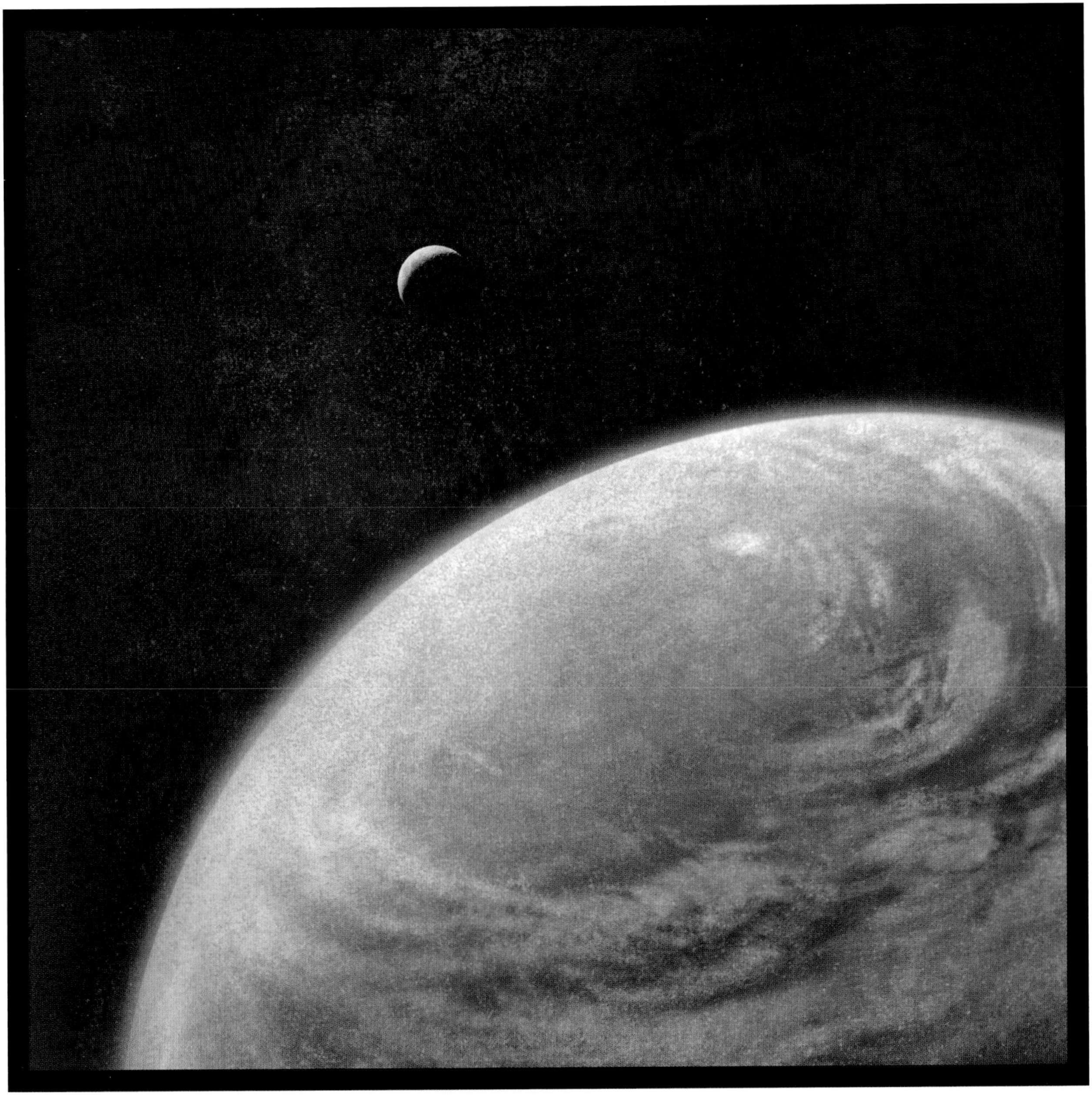

Centuries passed.

Eons passed.

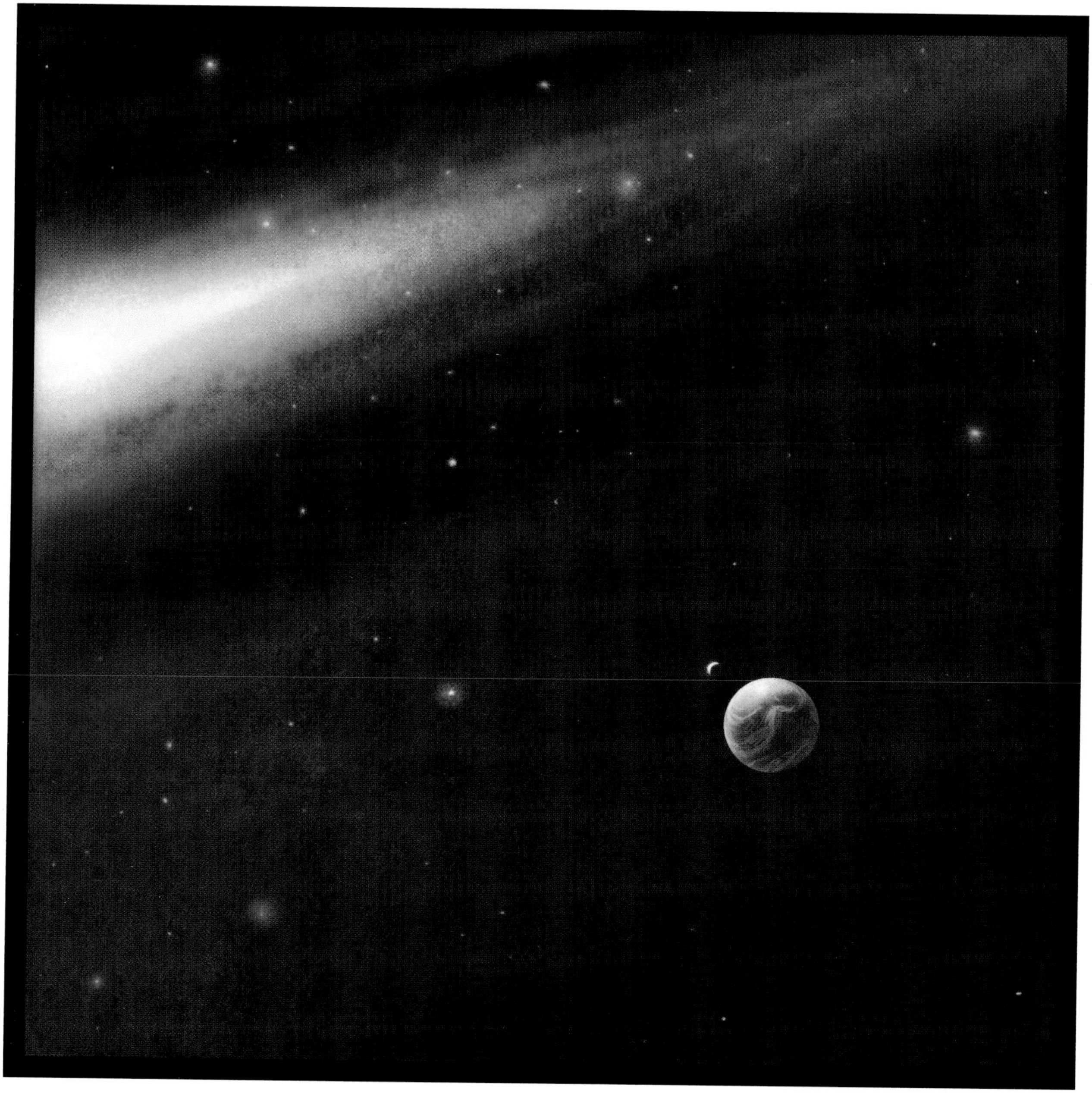

The universe
continued as usual.

And the Mysteries
lived happily ever after.

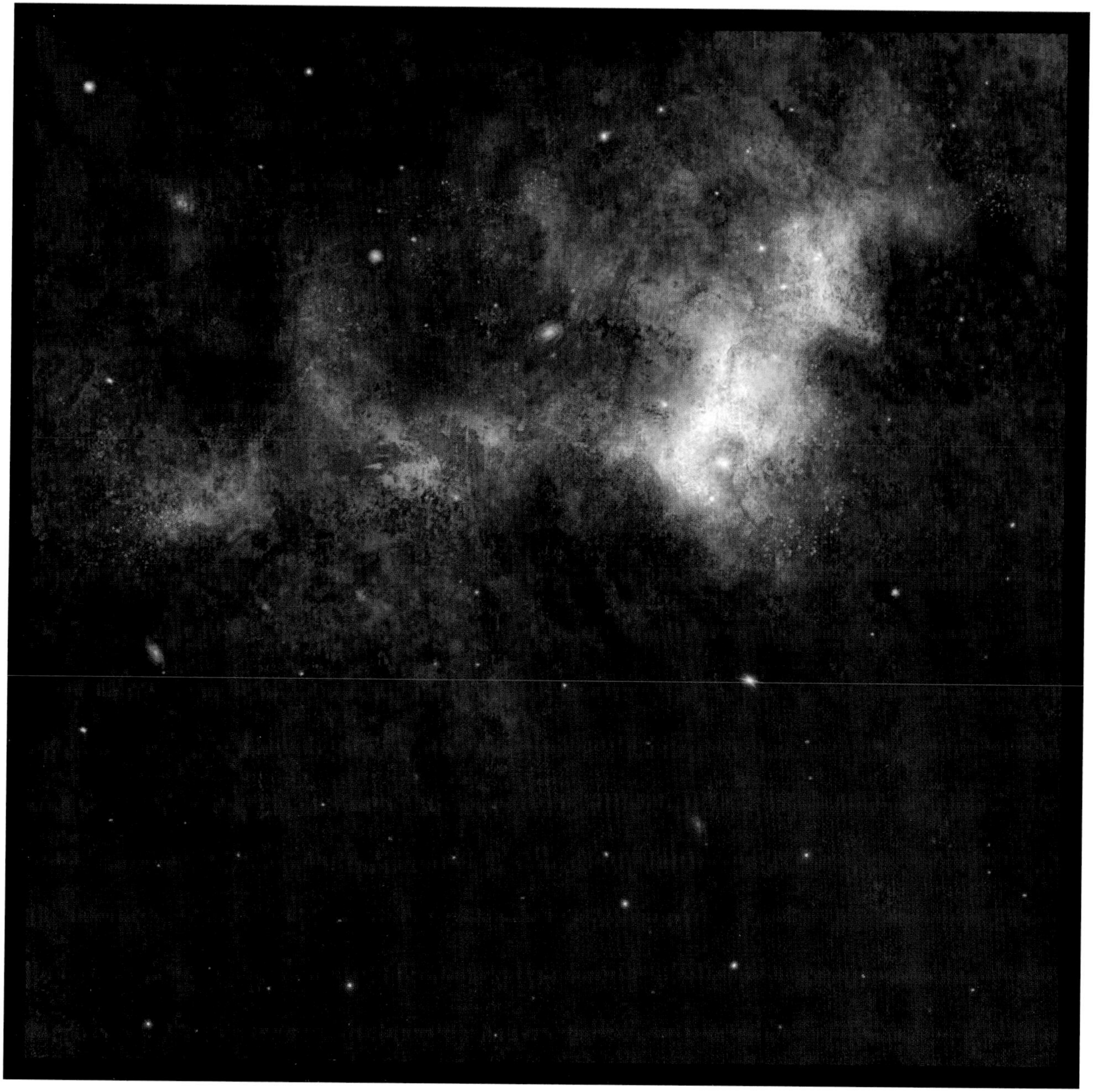